Closely KNIT

HANDMADE GIFTS
FOR THE ONES YOU LOVE

Hannah Fettig

NORTH LIGHT BOOKS
Cincinnati, OH

12 11 10 09 08   5 4 3 2 1

Distributed in Canada by Fraser Direct
100 Armstrong Avenue
Georgetown, ON, Canada L7G 5S4
Tel: (905) 877-4411

Distributed in the U.K. and Europe by David & Charles
Brunel House, Newton Abbot, Devon, TQ12 4PU, England
Tel: (+44) 1626 323200, Fax: (+44) 1626 323319
E-mail: postmaster@davidandcharles.co.uk

Distributed in Australia by Capricorn Link
P.O. Box 704, S. Windsor, NSW 2756 Australia
Tel: (02) 4577-3555
Library of Congress Cataloging-in-Publication Data

Fettig, Hannah.
    Closely knit : handmade gifts for the ones you love / By Hannah Fettig.
        p. cm.
    Includes index.
    ISBN-13: 978-1-60061-018-9
    1. Knitting--Patterns. 2. Gifts. I. Title.
TT820.F484 2008
746.43'2--dc22

2007036563

METRIC CONVERSION CHART

TO CONVERT	TO	MULTIPLY BY
Inches	Centimeters	2.54
Centimeters	Inches	0.4
Feet	Centimeters	30.5
Centimeters	Feet	0.03
Yards	Meters	0.9
Meters	Yards	1.1
Sq. Inches	Sq. Centimeters	6.45
Sq. Centimeters	Sq. Inches	0.16
Sq. Feet	Sq. Meters	0.09
Sq. Meters	Sq. Feet	10.8
Sq. Yards	Sq. Meters	0.8
Sq. Meters	Sq. Yards	1.2
Pounds	Kilograms	0.45
Kilograms	Pounds	2.2
Ounces	Grams	28.3
Grams	Ounces	0.035

fw
F+W PUBLICATIONS, INC.
www.fwpublications.com

Editor: JESSICA GORDON
Designer: MAYA DROZDZ
Production Coordinator: GREG NOCK
Photographer: BRIAN STEEGE
Cover Photographer: RIC DELIANTONI
Stylist: NORA MARTINI
Hair + Makeup: CASS SMITH

Dedication

In memory of my mother, Lauren Marie King

Acknowledgments
Or a Brief History of How This Book Happened

Thank you to my grandmother, June Smith, for showing us kids from a young age that crafts are wonderful and that they can certainly be a way of life.

Thank you to my high school art teacher, Rush Brown, for making me feel like everything I did was brilliant.

Thank you to Jeannine Kertzman for coming into my life when you did. I love you and all the paint and fabric and clay that comes with you, and one day you will get a decent mold of my face!

Thank you to Anna Poe and Josh Eckels for opening Knitwit Yarn Shop. I remember when I was first coming around the store, Anna asked me, "Do you ever think about designing your own stuff?" and I believe I said no. Well, look what's happened! You two have helped me in so many ways, and I thank you for being there for me as I took my knitting to the next level.

Thank you to Daphne and Iaian of The Fibre Company for having me along to TNNA that one summer, where I met the editor for this publication, and for providing all the yarn you did.

Thank you to Judy Warde for being a sounding board as this book tried to decide what it was doing, and also to Toby, the cutest dog in the world.

And thank you to Jessica Gordon, my fabulous editor. You made this, dare I say it, easy! I loved working with you.

How could I have done this without *all my knitters*?!!

First, in a great big way, I must thank my aunt, Lynn Cooke. I seriously do not know what I would have done without your passion, and the enthusiasm of your knitting guild, for getting these projects knit.

Of the Nashoba Valley Knitter's Guild, I wish to thank: Barbara Meyer, Maryanne Cleary, Lorri Wurtzler, Sandi MeyoPhoeter, Sue Dalton, Fran Meyers, Liz Barnhart, Linda Kiurla, Elizabeth Burns and Sheilah Johnson.

Next, I must thank Mo Fettig, my supportive mother-in-law, who took on the largest project...and had it done before any of the others!

Darlene Thompson, thank you for helping me out with knitting, and for the embroidery tutorial!

Aldona O. Shumway, thank you, thank you, thank you for picking up my half-knit projects and finishing them off beautifully, and thank you also to your son, Youssef Ayad.

To all those who have been supportive while I worked on this project:

Thank you to my dad, Richard, for letting us raid your candy drawer...and fridge and cupboards, especially during this project—no time to cook!

Thank you to my brother, David. Poor David has been trying to find a place to sit in my house his whole life, only to discover more knitting, knitting, knitting. Oh, and I really do just have one more row, then we can do that thing we talked about.

Thank you to my sister, Theresa. Please don't kill me for writing as much as I did about you in this book.

Thank you to my in-laws, Mo and Pete Fettig. You have been so supportive of Abe and me in all our ventures, and we feel blessed in this.

Thank you to my sister-in-law, Nellie. Where are you, anyway? Thanks for taking me to Knitwit for the first time.

Thank you to my aunts, Sheri and Ann, for always showing a special interest in whatever I am working on.

Thank you to Colleen and Dayna for being understanding when I couldn't come out to play because I had to knit 24/7!

And most of all, thank you to Abe. I appreciate your being supportive of my obsession with knitting. Throughout this project, you were so understanding, even with the all-night work sessions and the lack of home-cooked meals. I love you, and I love our life.

Contents

Introduction

HANDMADE GIFTS ARE THE BEST KIND TO GIVE AND RECEIVE. Better than anything you can buy in a store, they can be the best expression of the love and care you feel for the most important people in your life. Of course, they can also be last-minute disasters, and—worst-case scenario—they can completely miss the mark.

This book is filled with knitted gifts to perfectly fit all the people you love: special handknits for mothers, daughters, sisters, the men in your life, precious wee ones and treasured friends. You'll also find both small projects and more involved handknits, depending on how much time you have to invest in a gift. Easier and quicker options are also provided throughout the book for when your best-laid plans go awry (as best-laid plans often do).

Each of the projects in this book was designed and knitted with a specific person in mind. I thought about what that person would like, and I found inspiration in the details of his or her personality and lifestyle. As I thought of all the people I knit for, it made me think about how we have our actual families and then we have people who fill the roles of different family members in our lives. I lost my mother to cancer when I was in my early twenties. Since then, I've really cherished the women who have come into my life and who have helped to fill this role. A gift for one of these special people has to be handmade, created specifically for the person who will receive it.

I want the gifts I give my family and friends to mean something. I want the recipients to like what I've made—no, I want them to love it. If you are the crafty type, which you probably are if you are reading this, you know you have a whole world of possibilities at your fingertips. Sometimes that can create a barrier that is hard to overcome: too many options. I hope that within these pages you will find something to pour your creative gift-giving energy into. You will find projects such as the *Tree of Love Wall Hanging* (see page 46) and the *Embroidered Flower Socks* (see page 56) that allow room for self-expression. You have the opportunity to put your personal mark on whatever you knit to make a truly one-of-a-kind gift.

And when you knit up one of these patterns, the recipient won't be the only one who takes joy in your creativity. Knitting the projects in this book will be a pleasure to you as well. All of the projects use yarns that are lovely to work with and that knit up into a luxurious finished fabric. Some patterns call for yarns with fabulous hands, such as the combination of The Fibre Company's Khroma and Rowan's Kidsilk Haze used for the *Lace-Tipped Striped Scarf* (see page 28). Some yarns were selected for their beautiful shine, such as the Alpaca with a Twist Fino used for the *Vintage Knee Socks* (see page 32) or the Classic Elite Premiere used for the *Bird's Nest Pincushion* (see page 10). Of course, one of the most exciting parts of starting a project is choosing your supplies, so feel free to substitute one of your favorite yarns for those suggested, with correct gauge, of course.

I wish you the best on your handmade gift-making!

Time Guide

Sometimes you can plan out your gift-making schedule months or even an entire year in advance. And sometimes you realize you'd like to knit up a handmade gift with only days or weeks before the occasion. *Closely Knit* has patterns that fit all your time constraints. I've rated each pattern with hourglasses according to how long it will take to knit. Following is a general guideline.

1 Hourglass:
Look for the projects marked with one hourglass if you want something you can easily knit up in an afternoon (or at least in a single day).

2 Hourglasses:
A two-hourglass project might take you a few days to knit, depending on your level of intensity, of course.

3 Hourglasses:
Then there are those projects that will take some serious hunkering down to get through. Expect at least a few weeks of dedicated knitting to finish these projects.

Mothers

BOTH MY MOTHER AND MY GRANDMOTHER PASSED DOWN TO ME A LOVE FOR CRAFTS. They were always up to something involving either yarn, fabric or a hot glue gun. I also have a friend, Jeannine, who has been a strong mother figure in my life. She lives to create things and is constantly changing her surroundings in new and interesting ways. When I think about all of these maternal figures, I want to make them something by hand, because I know they will 100 percent appreciate the work and creative energy that goes into a handmade gift.

If your mother is a crafter, what a great gift the *Bird's Nest Pincushion* (see page 10) could be. It can be perched in a most special place.

If you've always wanted to knit your mother a sweater, I hope you will love the cardigan in this chapter (see page 22). It is cozy, feminine and very flattering. I thought of Jeannine when I made the sweater, and I knew she would appreciate the interesting detail at the cuffs and waist, as well as the bell-shaped sleeves.

My grandmother is crazy about photographs. Her love of family photos inspired the knit frame hung from a lovely ribbon (see page 14).

What mother doesn't deserve something in cashmere? Try knitting up the ruffly scarf in this chapter in her favorite color (see page 20). A knit pillow could be a great addition to your mother's sitting area— so easy to display and admire (see page 18).

I hope you find something in this chapter that can give you a sense of pride when you create it and hand it to this most important person.

Bird's Nest Pincushion

THIS LITTLE NEST CRADLES FIVE EGGS, CREATING THE PERFECT SPOT FOR YOUR MOTHER'S PINS AND NEEDLES. It will be the perfect addition to her craft corner! Add a little bird pin to the nest for an extra touch of whimsy.

FINISHED MEASUREMENTS
approx 3¾" (10cm) in diameter x 1½" (4cm) deep

YARN
1 skein Classic Elite Premiere (pima cotton/Tencel blend, 50 g, 108 yds [99m]) in each of the foll colors:
   color #5275 Coconut (A)
   color #5291 Robin's Egg (B)

NEEDLES AND NOTIONS
size US 6 (4.0mm) double-pointed needles

scrap yarn for provisional cast on

markers

yarn needle

cable needle

polyester fiberfill

small decorative bird (optional)

GAUGE
5¼ sts = 1" (3cm) in St st

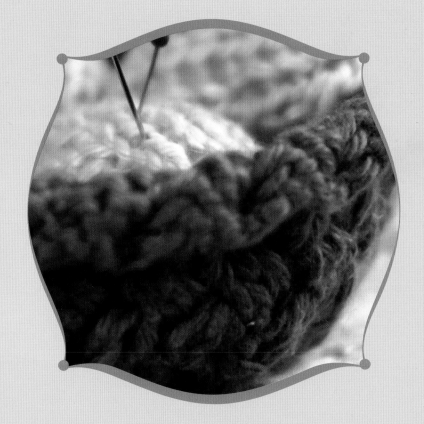

TECHNIQUES

C4B (CABLE 4 BACK): Slip 2 sts onto cn, hold cn in back of work, k2 from left needle, then k2 from cn to create a cable that crosses to the right.

C4F (CABLE 4 FRONT): Slip 2 sts onto cn, hold cn in front of work, k2 from left needle, then k2 from cn to create a cable that crosses to the left.

K2TOG (KNIT 2 TOGETHER): Dec 1 st by knitting 2 sts tog.

Pincushion

NEST

With size US 6 (4.0mm) DPNs and yarn A, cast on 90 sts. Join for working in the rnd, taking care not to twist sts.

ROWS 1–2: Knit.

ROW 3: * C4B; rep from * around, ending k2.

ROW 4: Knit.

ROW 5: K2, * C4F; rep from * to end.

ROW 6: Knit.

ROWS 7–14: Rep Rows 3–6 twice more.

ROWS 15–17: Rep Rows 3–5 once.

ROW 18 (DEC ROW): K3, * k2tog, k2; rep from * around, ending k3—69 sts.

ROW 19: * C4B, k2; rep from * around, ending k3.

ROW 20: K3 * k2tog twice, k2; rep from * to end—47 sts.

ROW 21: K2 * C4F; rep from * around, ending k1.

ROW 22: K2tog around, ending k1—24 sts.

ROW 23: Knit.

ROW 24: K2tog around—12 sts.

Cut the yarn, leaving a tail. Pull the tail through rem sts. Weave in all ends.

EGGS (MAKE 5)

Using a provisional cast on and size US 6 (4.0 mm) DPNs, CO 12 sts with yarn B. Divide sts evenly on 3 needles. Join for working in the rnd, pm at beg of rnd.

ଏ NOTE ଏ

To work a provisional cast on, crochet a chain with scrap yarn several chains longer than the number of sts you will be casting on. Cut yarn and tie off crochet chain. Leaving a tail, knit the number of cast-on sts indicated in the patt through the back loops of the crochet chain.

RNDS 1–4: Knit—12 sts.

RND 5: * K2, k2tog; rep from * around—9 sts.

RND 6: * K1, k2tog; rep from * around—6 sts.

ANOTHER GIFT IDEA
Add a bit of potpourri in with some of the polyester fiberfill in the eggs to give the pincushion your mother's favorite scent.

Break the yarn, leaving a tail. Thread the tail onto a yarn needle and pull tail tight through rem 6 sts. Weave the tail into the wrong side of the egg.

With yarn B, pick up 12 sts from the provisional cast on. Divide sts evenly on 3 needles. Pm at beg of rnd.

✂ NOTE ✂

To pick up sts from a provisional cast on, "unzip" the scrap yarn from the sts and slide each st onto a DPN as you pull away the scrap yarn. You may need to cut the crochet chain to release the sts. Make sure sts slide onto needle facing the right way.

RNDS 1–2: Knit—12 sts.

RND 3: * K2, k2tog; rep from * around—9 sts.

RNDS 4–6: Knit.

RND 7: * K1, k2tog; rep from * around—6 sts.

Break the yarn, leaving a tail. Thread the tail onto a yarn needle.

Stuff the egg with polyester fiberfill.

Pull the tail tight through rem sts. Weave in all ends.

FINISHING

Fill the nest with eggs. Attach eggs to inside of nest with yarn needle and yarn B.

Add decorative bird, if desired.

QUICK FIX
*Very short on time?
Purchase a small wicker
or wooden bowl to cradle
knit eggs.*

Lacy Hanging Picture Frame

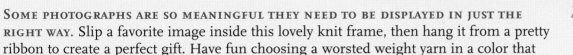

SOME PHOTOGRAPHS ARE SO MEANINGFUL THEY NEED TO BE DISPLAYED IN JUST THE RIGHT WAY. Slip a favorite image inside this lovely knit frame, then hang it from a pretty ribbon to create a perfect gift. Have fun choosing a worsted weight yarn in a color that complements the image to be displayed. For a soft black-and-white image, a blend in a soft shade works well. For a bright, colorful image, choose a complementary or neutral shade in a smooth yarn that will create a sharp outline.

FINISHED MEASUREMENTS
Outer edge: 5½" x 7½" (14cm x 19cm)

Frame opening: 2" x 4" (5cm x 10cm)

YARN
1 skein Rowan Kid Classic (lambswool/kid mohair/nylon blend, 50 g, 153 yds [140m])
   color #841 Lavender Ice

NEEDLES AND NOTIONS
16" (40cm) size US 7 (4.5mm) circular needle

size US H/8 (5.0mm) crochet hook

yarn needle

approx 8" (20cm) of ribbon

sewing needle

sewing thread

GAUGE
20 sts x 24 rows = 4" (10cm) in St st

TECHNIQUES

SSK (SLIP, SLIP, KNIT): Dec 1 st by slipping 2 sts knitwise one at a time from the left needle to the right needle. Insert the tip of the left needle into the front of both sts and knit the 2 sts tog.

K2TOG (KNIT 2 TOGETHER): Dec 1 st by knitting 2 sts tog.

YO (YARN OVER): Wrap the working yarn around the needle clockwise, and knit the next st as usual. This operation creates an eyelet hole in the knitting and inc 1 st.

SL ST (SLIP STITCH): Insert the tip of the right needle into the first st on the left needle purlwise and slip the st from the left needle to the right needle without knitting it.

Frame

With size US 7 (4.5mm) circular needle, CO 126 sts. Join for working in the rnd, taking care not to twist sts. Pm at beg of rnd.

RND 1: K36, pm, k27, pm, k36, pm, k27—126 sts.

RND 2: * K1, SSK, knit to 3 sts before next marker, k2tog, k1, sm; rep from * to end of rnd—118 sts.

RND 3: Knit.

Rep Rnds 2–3 five times more, or until frame opening is desired size—78 sts.

BO all sts.

BACK

BOTTOM FLAP

With size US 7 (4.5mm) needles, CO 25 sts. Work in St st until piece measures 4" (10cm). BO.

TOP FLAP

With size US 7 (4.5 mm) needles, CO 25 sts. Work in St st until piece measures 4½" (11cm), ending with a WS row.

TURNING RIDGE (RS): Purl.

Work 6 rows in St st.

BO sts. Turn facing under along turning ridge. Stitch into place.

FINISHING

With wrong sides tog, place top flap over bottom flap and join flaps to back of frame with mattress st. See the Glossary, page 141, for instructions on working in mattress st.

Using a crochet hook, work a picot edge around the outer and inner edges of the frame as foll: Using a size H/8 (5.0mm) crochet hook, join yarn with sl st in any st. * Chain 3 (Ch3), sl st in same st as last sl st (picot made), sl st in each of next 3 sts, rep from * to end. Join with sl st in beg sl st. Fasten off.

Sew ribbon to back of frame to form hanging loop.

❧ NOTE ❧

Depending on the yarn you use, you may want to insert an appropriate size mat into the frame to give it added structure.

Mohair-Blend Square Pillow

THIS COMFY SQUARE PILLOW IS AN ATTRACTIVE ADDITION TO ANY MOTHER'S HOME. As you choose the colors for your mother's pillow, think about where she has focused her decorating powers. Does she have a favorite sitting area? Is her bedroom her haven of relaxation? Pick colors that complement her current decorations. I designed this soft cushion with one of my favorite yarns, Rowan Kid Classic. It is so rich-looking and comes in beautiful shades. With time, it acquires a nice halo from just the right amount of mohair blended with lambswool.

FINISHED MEASUREMENTS
16" x 16" (41cm x 41cm)

YARN
2 skeins Rowan Kid Classic (lambswool/kid mohair/nylon blend, 50 g, 153 yds [140m])
   color #853 Spruce (MC)

1 skein Rowan Kid Classic in each of the foll colors:
   color #845 Battle (CC1)
   color #832 Peat (CC2)

NEEDLES AND NOTIONS
size US 8 (5.0mm) circular or straight needles

16" x 16" (41cm x 41cm) pillow form

yarn needle

GAUGE
18 sts x 24 rows = 4" (10cm) in St st

Pillow

BACK
With size US 8 (5.0mm) needles and MC, CO 73 sts. Work in St st until piece measures 16" (41cm) from cast-on edge. BO all sts.

FRONT

✑ NOTE ✑
Work the striped color block in intarsia, using separate balls of MC for the left and right edges. Always twist the yarns at the color change to prevent holes at the edges of the color-block design.

With size US 8 (5.0mm) needles and MC, CO 73 sts. Work in St st for 14 rows, or until piece measures 2⅜" (6cm) from cast-on edge, ending with a WS row.

ROW 1 (RS): K9 with MC (drop first ball of MC), k55 with CC1, k9 with second ball of MC.

ROW 2 (WS): P9 with MC, p55 with CC1, p9 with MC.

ROW 3: K9 with MC, k55 with CC2, k9 with MC.

ROW 4: P9 with MC, p55 with CC2, p9 with MC.

ROW 5: K9 with MC, k55 with CC1, k9 with MC.

ROW 6: P9 with MC, k55 with CC1, p9 with MC.

ROW 7: Knit with MC.

ROW 8: Purl with MC.

Rep Rows 1–8 until piece measures 14" (36cm) from cast-on edge, ending with Row 6.

With MC, work in St st until entire piece measures 16" (41cm) from cast-on edge. BO all sts.

Block front and back of pillow.

FINISHING
Attach front to back, sewing the sides with vertical-to-vertical mattress st, and using horizontal-to-horizontal mattress st along the top. See the Glossary, page 141, for instructions on working in mattress st.

Insert pillow form. Sew up rem side with horizontal-to-horizontal mattress st.

Cashmere Ruffles Scarf

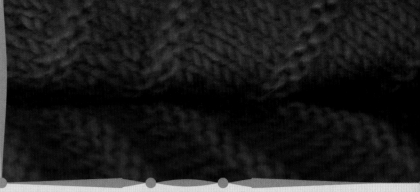

YOUR MOM DESERVES A LITTLE CASHMERE IN HER LIFE. Try this fun-to-knit scarf featuring short rows knit with Karabella Boise, a cashmere and wool blend. As you knit, watch it take its organic, kelp-like shape. This scarf will dress up the simplest of outfits, and when people ooh and ahh she can gladly say, "My daughter made it."

FINISHED MEASUREMENTS
approx 8" x 51" (20cm x 130cm)

YARN
4 skeins Karabella Yarns Boise (cashmere/merino wool blend, 50 g, 163 yds [150m])
   color #63 Wine Red

NEEDLES AND NOTIONS
size US 5 (3.75mm) needles

yarn needle

GAUGE
24 sts x 32 rows = 4" (10cm) in St st

TECHNIQUES
SHORT ROW SHAPING
(RS) WRAP AND TURN (W&T): Wyif, sl 1 st from the left needle to the right. Move the yarn to the back, sl st back to the left needle, turn work. 1 st has been wrapped.

(WS) WRAP AND TURN (W&T): Wyib, sl 1 st from the left needle to the right. Move the yarn to the front, sl st back to the left needle, turn work. 1 st has been wrapped.

❧ NOTE ❧
Whenever you come to a wrap, work the wrap tog with the st it wraps. To pick up a wrap and its st, slide the tip of the right needle into the wrap from the front of the work and place the wrap on the left needle alongside the st it wraps. Knit the 2 loops tog as one st.

Scarf

With size US 5 (3.75mm) needles, CO 55 sts.

Purl 1 row.

Knit 1 row.

BEGIN PATTERN STITCH

ROW 1 (RS): K22, w&t.

ROW 2: P22.

ROW 3: K24, w&t.

ROW 4: P24.

ROWS 5–6: Rep Rows 1–2.

ROW 7: K25, p5, k25.

ROW 8 (WS): P22, w&t.

ROW 9: K22.

ROW 10: P24, w&t.

ROW 11: K24.

ROWS 12–13: Rep Rows 8–9.

ROW 14: P25, k5, p25.

ROW 15 (RS): Purl.

ROW 16: Knit.

Rep Rows 1–16 of pattern stitch until scarf reaches desired length.

BO all sts. Weave in ends.

ANOTHER GIFT IDEA
With any fall or winter accessory, take into consideration the color of the jacket the recipient usually wears, and coordinate the color of the scarf to match it. Also consider the tastes and predilections of the giftee—just because you like tangerine doesn't mean your mother does.

Cabled Cardigan

OF COURSE, YOUR MOTHER WOULD BE HAPPY TO WEAR ANY SWEATER YOU KNIT FOR HER, NO MATTER HOW OVERSIZED AND SHAPELESS. But I kept her feminine side in mind when I created this cozy cardigan knit in an alpaca-and-wool blend yarn. Lovely ruffles grace the hemline and cuffs. The contoured waist is mimicked in the bell-shaped sleeves, and a handsome cable climbs the center back of the sweater.

SIZES
S (M , L)

To fit actual bust sizes: 36 (38, 40)" (91 [97, 102]cm)

FINISHED MEASUREMENTS
Chest measurement: 40 (41¾, 44)" (102 [106, 112]cm)

Length: 26½ (27½, 27¾)" 67 (70, 70)cm

Sleeve from shoulder to underarm: 17¾ (18, 18¼)" (45 [46, 46]cm)

YARN
13 (15, 17) skeins The Fibre Company Babe
(baby alpaca/merino wool blend, 50 g, 100 yds [91m])
   color Poppy

NEEDLES AND NOTIONS
24" (61cm) size US 7 (4.5mm) circular needle

24" (61cm) size US 2 (2.75 mm) circular needle

yarn needle

10 shell buttons, ⅝" (2cm) in diameter

GAUGE
20 sts x 28 rows = 4" (10cm) in St st with larger size needle

↩ NOTE ↪
Row gauge is very important in this pattern because the buttonholes are knitted in as you knit the right front. Be sure to change needle size, if necessary, to achieve the correct stitch and row gauge.

TECHNIQUES
C4B (CABLE 4 BACK): Slip 2 sts to cn and hold to the back of the work. K2, k2 from cn.

C4F (CABLE 4 FRONT): Slip 2 sts to cn and hold to the front of the work. K2, k2 from cn.

SSK (SLIP, SLIP, KNIT): Dec 1 st by slipping 2 sts knitwise one at a time from the left needle to the right needle. Insert the tip of the left needle into the front of both sts and knit the 2 sts tog.

M1 (MAKE 1 PURLWISE): Inc 1 st by picking up, from back to front, the bar between the next st and the st just knit and placing it on the left needle. Knit into the front of the picked-up st.

K2TOG (KNIT 2 TOGETHER): Dec 1 st by knitting 2 sts tog.

P2TOG (PURL 2 TOGETHER): Dec 1 st by purling 2 sts tog.

WORK 2 TOG (KNIT OR PURL 2 TOGETHER): Dec 1 st by knitting or purling 2 sts tog as one, in keeping with est patt.

YO (YARN OVER): Wrap the working yarn around the needle clockwise, and knit the next st as usual. This operation creates an eyelet hole in the knitting and inc 1 st.

23

BACK

With size US 7 (4.5mm) needles, cast on 212 (220, 232) sts. Beg with a purl row, work in St st for 5 rows.

Switch to US size 2 (2.75 mm) needles.

* K2tog; rep from * across row—106 (110, 116) sts.

Purl 1 row. Switch to size US 7 (4.5mm) needles.

BEGIN BACK CENTER CABLE PATTERN (8-ROW REP)

ROW 1: K46 (48, 51), p1, C4B, p1, k46 (48, 51).

ROWS 2, 4, 6 AND 8: P46 (48, 51), k1, p12, k1, p46 (48, 51).

ROW 3: K46 (48, 51), p1, k12, p1, k46 (48, 51).

ROW 5: K46 (48, 51), p1, C4F, p1, k46 (48, 51).

ROW 7: Rep Row 3.

∾ NOTE ∾
Cont to work 8 rows of cable pattern to top of back.

Work even in est patt, until piece measures 2¾ (2¾, 3)" (7 [7, 8]cm), ending with a WS row.

DEC ROW (RS): K2, SSK, work to last 4 sts, k2tog, k2—104 (108, 114) sts.

Rep dec row every 4th row 9 (11, 11) times more, and every 6th row 1 (0, 0) time(s)—84 (86, 92) sts.

Work even for 7 rows, ending with a WS row.

INC ROW (RS): K2, m1, work to last 2 sts, m1, k2—86 (88, 94) sts.

Rep inc row every 6th row 7 (3, 3) times, then every 4th row 1 (6, 6) time(s)—102 (106, 112) sts.

Cont straight until piece measures 17 (17¼, 17¾)" 43 (18, 20)cm from beg, ending with a WS row.

BEGIN ARMHOLE SHAPING

BO 7 (8, 9) sts at beg of next 2 rows—88 (90, 94) sts.

DEC ROW: K2, SSK, work to last 4 sts, k2tog, k2—86 (88, 92) sts.

Work dec row EOR 4 (4, 5) times, then every 4th row 3 (3, 3) times—72 (74, 76) sts.

Cont straight until armhole measures 8¼ (8½, 8⅝)" 21 (22, 22)cm.

BEGIN NECK AND SHOULDER SHAPING
Beg with a RS row, BO 3 (4, 5) sts, knit to end, placing center 14 sts on a holder for neck. Work left shoulder first:

ROW 1 (WS): BO 3 (4, 5) sts at beg of row, purl to neck edge—26 sts.

ROWS 2–3: BO 4 sts at beg of these 2 rows—18 sts.

ROW 4 (RS): BO 3 sts at beg of row—15 sts.

ROW 5: BO 4 sts at beg of row—11 sts.

ROW 6: K2, SSK, knit to end—10 sts

ROW 7: BO 5 sts at beg of row—5 sts.

ROW 8: BO rem 5 sts.

Work right shoulder as foll: With WS facing, attach yarn at neck edge.

ROWS 1–2: BO 4 sts at beg of these 2 rows—18 sts.

ROW 3 (WS): BO 3 sts at beg of row—15 sts.

ROW 4: BO 4 sts at beg of row—11 sts.

ROW 5 (WS): P2, p2tog, purl to end—10 sts.

ROW 6: BO 5 sts at beg of next row—5 sts.

ROW 7: BO rem 5 sts.

LEFT FRONT
With size US 7 (4.5mm) needle, cast on 115 (119, 125) sts.

ROWS 1 AND 3: Purl.

ROW 2: Knit to last 5 sts, sl 1, k4.

ROWS 4–5: Rep Rows 2–3.

Switch to size US 2 (2.75mm) needle. * K2tog; rep from * to last 5 sts, sl 1, k4— 60 (62, 65) sts. Purl 1 row.

Switch to size US 7 (4.5mm) needles. Work in St st. On every knit row, work last 5 sts as foll for button band facing: sl 1, k4.

Work even in St st until piece measures 2¾ (2¾, 3)" (7 [7, 8]cm) from beg, ending with a WS row.

DEC ROW (RS): K2, SSK, work to end of row—59 (61, 64) sts.

Rep dec row every 4th row 9 (11, 11) times more, and every 6th row 1 (0, 0) time(s)— 49 (50, 53) sts.

Work even for 7 rows, ending with a WS row.

INC ROW (RS): K2, m1, work to end—50 (51, 54) sts.

Rep inc row every 6th row 7 (3, 3) times, then every 4th row 1 (6, 6) time(s)—58 (60, 63) sts.

Cont straight until piece measures 17 (17¼, 17¾)" 43 (44, 45)cm from beg, ending with a WS row.

BEGIN ARMHOLE SHAPING
Beg with a RS row, BO 7 (8, 9) sts, work to end—51 (52, 54) sts. Purl 1 row.

DEC ROW: K2, SSK, work to end—50 (51, 53) sts.

Work dec row EOR 4 (4, 5) times more, then every 4th row 3 (3, 3) times—43 (44, 45) sts.

Cont straight until armhole measures 6¼ (6½, 6½)" (16 [17, 17]cm), ending with a RS row.

BEGIN NECK SHAPING

ROW 1 (WS): BO 8, purl to end—35 (36, 37) sts.

ROWS 2, 4 AND 6: Knit.

ROW 3: BO 4, purl to end—31 (32, 33) sts.

ROW 5: BO 3, purl to end—28 (29, 30) sts.

ROW 7: BO 3, purl to end—25 (26, 27) sts.

ROW 8 (RS): Knit to last 4 sts, k2tog, k2—24 (25, 26) sts.

Rep dec row at neck edge EOR 3 times more—21 (22, 23) sts.

BEGIN SHOULDER SHAPING

ROW 1 (RS): BO 3 (4, 5), knit to end—18 sts.

ROWS 2, 4 AND 6: Purl.

ROWS 3 AND 5: BO 4 at the beg of these 2 rows, knit to end—10 sts.

ROW 7: BO 5, knit to end—5 sts.

ROW 8: Bind off rem 5 sts.

RIGHT FRONT

Work the same as left front, reversing shaping. Work buttonholes in as foll: Beg 2⅝ (2¾, 2⅞)" (7 [7, 7]cm) from bottom, create buttonhole: (RS) K2tog, yo, k2, s1, k2, yo, k2tog, work to end.

Create buttonholes every 2¼" (6cm), or every 16th row—10 buttonholes total.

SLEEVES (MAKE 2)

With size US 7 (4.5mm) needle, CO 140 (144, 144) sts. Purl 1 row.

Work in St st for 4 rows.

With size US 2 (2.75mm) needle, k2tog across row—70 (72, 72) sts.

Purl 1 row.

With US size 7 (4.5 mm) needle, work in St st until work measures 4" (10cm) from cast-on edge, ending with a WS row.

DEC ROW (RS): K2, SSK, knit to last 4 sts, k2tog, k2—68 (70, 70) sts.

Work dec row every 6th row 5 times more—58 (60, 60) sts.

Work 5 (7, 9) rows even, ending with a WS row.

INC ROW: K2, m1, work to last 2 sts, m1, k2—60 (62, 62) sts.

Rep inc row every 6th row 5 (5, 6) times, then every 8th row twice—74 (76, 78) sts.

Cont straight until sleeve measures 17¾ (18, 18¼)" (45 [46, 46]cm).

BEGIN CAP SHAPING

BO 7 (8, 9) sts at beg of next 2 rows—60 (60, 60) sts.

DEC ROW: K2, SSK, work to last 4 sts, k2tog, k2—58 sts.

Rep dec row EOR 15 times more—28 sts.

BO 2 sts at beg of next 4 rows—20 sts.

BO rem 20 sts.

FINISHING

BUTTON BANDS

Turn facing in along turning ridge created by slipped st on left and right front pieces. Stitch into place, lining up buttonholes on right front. Attach buttons to left front to correspond to buttonholes on right front.

Join side, shoulder and sleeve seams using mattress st. See the Glossary, page 141, for instructions on working in mattress st. Ease sleeve caps into armholes.

ROLLED NECKLINE

With size US 7 (4.5mm) circular needle and with RS facing, pick up and knit an even number of sts, evenly spaced, around neck edge. Work in St st for 1" (3cm). BO loosely. Purl side of collar will roll to outside. Fasten in place or leave free.

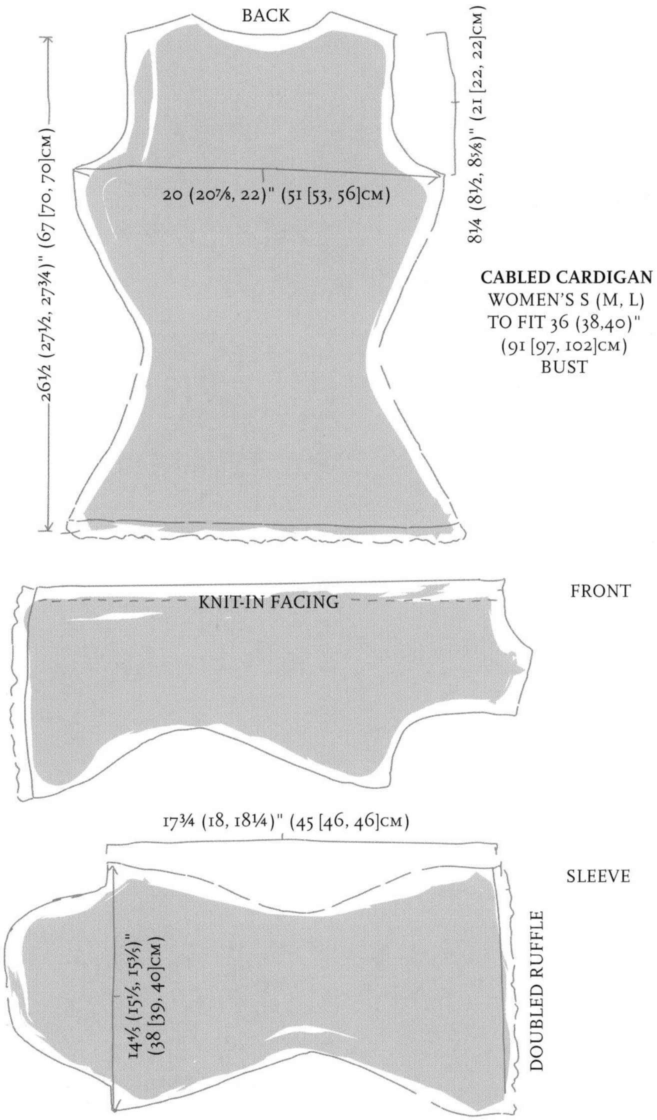
BACK
26½ (27½, 27¾)" (67 [70, 70]cm)
20 (20⅞, 22)" (51 [53, 56]cm)
8¼ (8½, 8⅝)" (21 [22, 22]cm)
CABLED CARDIGAN
WOMEN'S S (M, L)
TO FIT 36 (38,40)"
(91 [97, 102]cm)
BUST
KNIT-IN FACING
FRONT
17¾ (18, 18¼)" (45 [46, 46]cm)
SLEEVE
14⅘ (15⅕, 15⅗)"
(38 [39, 40]cm)
DOUBLED RUFFLE

Daughters

WHEN CREATING THE PROJECTS IN THIS CHAPTER,
I THOUGHT ABOUT WHAT SORT OF KNIT GIFT I WOULD
WANT TO RECEIVE FROM MY MOTHER AS A YOUNG WOMAN
IN MY TWENTIES. I love alpaca, so you will find alpaca and
alpaca blends dominating the items in this chapter.
I also love boutique clothing, so the wearables are
inspired by the sorts of things I see when I shop at my
favorite stores. My grandmother is my predecessor in
handmade gift-giving. She has made countless gifts for
all her loved ones, including quilted wall hangings. I
have featured a knit version here that allows room for
your own personal touches (see the *Tree of Love Wall
Hanging*, page 46). The classic teddy bear (see page 36)
is included for young daughters—or for those who are
young at heart!

The lace-trimmed scarf and hat (see page 28), the
Vintage Knee Socks (see page 32) and the *Cap-Sleeved
Eyelet Top* (see page 42) will let mothers enjoy dressing
up their daughters all over again, like they did when we
were young. With this collection of pretty gifts to choose
from, you can be sure your daughter will actually wear
or use what you knit for her.

Lace-Tipped Striped Scarf and Hat

THIS VIBRANTLY COLORED HAT AND SCARF WITH DELICATE LACE DETAIL AT THE ENDS WILL KEEP YOUR PRECIOUS BABY GIRL (EVEN IF SHE IS ALL GROWN UP) WARM AND STYLISH ALL WINTER LONG. The combination of a lace-weight mohair yarn with a dk weight alpaca-and-merino blend creates a very touchable texture.

Scarf

FINISHED MEASUREMENTS
8" x 72" (20cm x 183cm)

YARN
2 skeins The Fibre Company Khroma DK
(baby alpaca/merino blend, 50 g, 160 yds [146m])
  color #05 Winesap (MC)

2 skeins Rowan Kidsilk Haze (super kid
mohair/silk blend, 25 g, 229 yds [210m])
  color #596 Marmalade (CC)

NEEDLES AND NOTIONS
16" (40cm) size US 4 (3.5mm) circular needle

yarn needle

GAUGE
24 sts x 32 rows = 4" (10cm) in St st, in stripe pattern

Hat

FINISHED MEASUREMENTS
approx 19½" (50cm) around x 8" (20cm)
tall with brim stretched out

One size fits most women.

YARN
1 skein The Fibre Company Khroma DK
(baby alpaca/merino blend, 50 g, 160 yds [146m])
  color #10 Night Sky (MC)

1 skein Rowan Kidsilk Haze (super kid
mohair/silk blend, 25 g, 229 yds [210m])
  color #585 Nightly (CC)

NEEDLES AND NOTIONS
size US 4 (3.5mm) double-pointed needles

yarn needle

GAUGE

Gauge same as for Scarf.

TECHNIQUES

SL ST (SLIP STITCH): Insert the tip of the right needle into the first st on the left needle purlwise and slip the st from the left needle to the right needle without knitting it.

PSSO (PASS SLIPPED ST OVER): Insert the tip of the left needle into the slipped st(s) on the right needle and slide it onto the left needle, bringing it over any knitted st(s) to dec.

K2TOG (KNIT 2 TOGETHER): Dec 1 st by knitting 2 sts tog.

K3TOG (KNIT 3 TOGETHER): Dec 2 sts by knitting 3 sts tog.

YO (YARN OVER): Wrap the working yarn around the needle clockwise, and knit the next st as usual. This operation creates an eyelet hole in the knitting and inc 1 st.

Hat

With MC and size US 4 (3.5mm) circular needle, CO 126 sts. Join for working in the rnd, taking care not to twist sts. Pm for beg of rnd.

Beg foll hat chart with Rnd 1, reading all rows of chart from right to left for circular knitting, and rep 18 sts of chart 7 times. Knit all odd-numbered rows of chart.

🙟 NOTE 🙜
All rnds of lace pattern will have 126 sts.

Work Rows 1–12 of chart with MC.

BEGIN COLOR STRIPE PATTERN
Beg with Row 13 of chart, * work 2 rnds with CC, then 2 rnds with MC, rep from * for color stripe pattern. AT THE SAME TIME cont to foll the chart for lace pattern from Row 13–24, carrying unused color lightly up the inside of hat at beg of rnd. Cont to work stripes through top of hat.

After completing the chart, cont to work in color stripe pattern as est, inc 2 sts evenly spaced on first rnd, until hat measures 5" (13cm) from cast-on edge—128 sts.

BEGIN DECREASING TO SHAPE TOP OF HAT

RND 1: * K6, k2tog; rep from * to end of rnd—112 sts.

RNDS 2–4: Knit.

RND 5: * K5, k2tog; rep from * to end of rnd—96 sts.

RNDS 6–8: Knit.

RND 9: * K4, k2tog; rep from * to end of rnd—80 sts.

RNDS 10–12: Knit.

RND 13: * K3, k2tog; rep from * to end of rnd—64 sts.

RNDS 14–16: Knit.

RND 17: * K2, k2tog; rep from * to end of rnd—48 sts.

RNDS 18–20: Knit.

RND 21: * K1, k2tog; rep from * to end of rnd—32 sts.

RND 22: * K2tog around—16 sts.

Break yarn, leaving a long tail. Thread the tail through a yarn needle and draw through rem sts, slipping them off the needle. Pull up tightly. Weave in all ends.

Scarf

SCARF HALF (MAKE 2)

🙟 NOTE 🙜
The scarf is knitted in 2 identical sections and then grafted at the center with Kitchener stitch.

**With MC and size US 4 (3.5mm) needles, CO 56 sts.

Purl 1 row.

Begin scarf chart with Row 1, reading odd-numbered (RS) rows from right to left.

Purl Row 2 (WS) and all subsequent even-numbered rows, reading the chart from left to right.

🙟 NOTE 🙜
All rows of lace pattern will have 56 sts.

Cont to work Rows 1–11 with MC.

BEGIN COLOR STRIPE PATTERN
Beg with Row 12 (WS), * work 2 rows with CC, then 2 rows with MC, rep from * for color stripe pattern, AT THE SAME TIME cont to foll the scarf chart from Row 12–35, carrying unused color lightly up the side of scarf.

After completing the chart, cont to work in color stripe pattern as est until 1 skein MC has been used up, ending with 1 row MC. Leave a long yarn tail for grafting. Place sts on a holder. Rep from ** to knit other half of scarf.

JOIN SCARF HALVES
Graft the 2 sections of the scarf tog with Kitchener st. See the Glossary, page 141, for instructions on grafting with Kitchener st.

HAT CHART

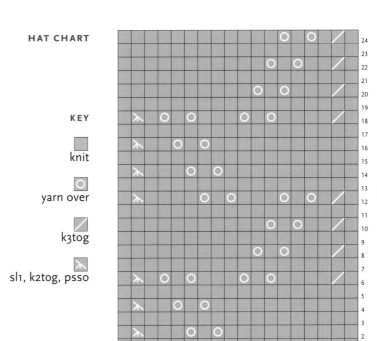

KEY

▨	knit
◉	yarn over
◨	k3tog
✈	sl1, k2tog, psso

SCARF CHART

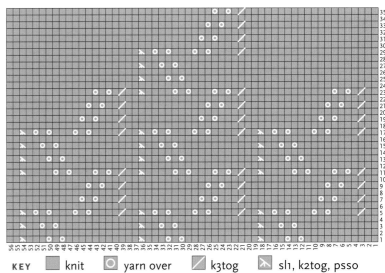

KEY   ▨ knit   ◉ yarn over   ◨ k3tog   ✈ sl1, k2tog, psso

Vintage Knee Socks

YOUR DAUGHTER WILL WANT TO PLAN A SPECIAL OUTFIT RIGHT AROUND THESE LOVELY, LOVELY KNEE SOCKS. Knit with a baby alpaca-and-silk blend yarn, they are soft and cozy with just enough shine. White lacy socks can be worn on special occasions with heels for everyone to enjoy. Or she can wear them as her little secret, under her jeans or in the comfort of home.

SIZES
The pattern as written is for a women's medium. Socks may easily be sized for a smaller or larger foot by changing needle size, and thus gauge, to change circumference. Length of foot may easily be adjusted by knitting foot section until 1¾" (4cm) short of your desired length, then starting toe shaping.

YARN
2 skeins Alpaca with a Twist Fino (baby alpaca/silk blend, 100 g, 875 yds [800m])
   color #0099 First Frost

✺ NOTE ✺
Work with 2 strands held tog throughout.

NEEDLES AND NOTIONS
size US 2 (2.75mm) double-pointed needles

size US 3 (3.25mm) double-pointed needles

markers

yarn needle

GAUGE
32 sts x 48 rows = 4" (10cm) in St st with 2 strands of yarn held tog, using larger needles

TECHNIQUES

K2TOG (KNIT 2 TOGETHER): Dec 1 st by knitting 2 sts tog.

P2TOG (PURL 2 TOGETHER): Dec 1 st by purling 2 sts tog.

SL (SLIP STITCH): Pass 1 st purlwise from left needle to right needle without knitting it.

SSK (SLIP, SLIP, KNIT): Dec 1 st by slipping 2 sts knitwise one at a time from the left needle to the right needle. Insert the tip of the left needle into the front of both sts and knit the 2 sts tog.

Socks (make 2)

With size US 2 (2.75mm) DPNs and 2 strands of yarn held tog, CO 72 sts. Divide evenly onto 3 needles. Join to work in the rnd, pm at beg of rnd. Work in k1, p1 ribbing for 2" (5cm).

INC RND: * Rib 18 sts, m1; rep from * to end of rnd— 4 sts inc, 76 sts total.

Switch to size US 3 (3.25mm) DPNs.

Work patt foll chart 1, beg with Row 1 and reading each row of chart from right to left for circular knitting. The diamond stitch pattern has a 19-st patt rep. There will be 4 full rep of the patt st around the sock. Complete chart 1, working Rows 1–42.

CHART 1

DEC RND: * P1, k3, p3, k3, p1, SSK, k4, k2tog; rep from * to end of rnd—68 sts.

ꙮ NOTE ꙮ
The diamond stitch pattern now has 17 sts for each rep.

CHART 2

Work 7 rows of chart 2 once.

DEC RND: * P1, k3, p3, k3, p1, SSK, k2, k2tog; rep from * to end of rnd—60 sts.

ꙮ NOTE ꙮ
The diamond stitch pattern now has 15 sts for each rep.

CHART 3

Foll Rows 1–7 of chart 3 until piece measures 12½" (32cm) from beg of sock, ending after a Row 1.

DIVIDE FOR HEEL

Remove marker. Place 30 sts on 1 needle, recentering sts so 4 St sts are at center of needle, with 1 diamond section on either side. Place rem sts on a holder for instep.

WORK HEEL

ROW 1 (RS): * Sl 1, k1; rep from * to end of row.

ROW 2 (WS): Sl 1, purl to end.

Rep Rows 1–2 for a total of 30 rows.

TURN HEEL

ROW 1: K16, SSK, k1, turn.

ROW 2: Sl 1, p4, p2tog, p1, turn.

ROW 3: Sl 1, k5, SSK, k1, turn.

ROW 4: Sl 1, p6, p2tog, p1, turn.

ROW 5: Sl 1, k7, SSK, k1, turn.

ROW 6: Sl 1, p8, p2tog, p1, turn.

ROW 7: Sl 1, k9, SSK, k1, turn.

ROW 8: Sl 1, p10, p2tog, p1, turn.

ROW 9: Sl 1, k11, SSK, k1, turn.

ROW 10: Sl 1, p12, p2tog, p1, turn.

ROW 11: Sl 1, k13, SSK, k1, turn.

ROW 12: Sl 1, p14, p2tog, p1, turn—18 sts.

Remove instep sts from holder and place on a needle.

GUSSET

(RS) Knit across heel sts.

With needle 1, pick up and knit 15 sts along selvage edge between heel and instep.

With needle 2, knit across 30 instep sts, working in St st.

With needle 3, pick up and knit 15 sts along rem selvage edge, and then knit across 9 sts of heel. You will have 9 sts on your left needle. Pm for beg of rnd, then slide these 9 sts onto needle 1. Heel sts are now divided between needles 1 and 3—78 sts total.

Knit 1 rnd even.

DEC RND

NEEDLE 1: Knit to last 3 sts, k2tog, k1.

NEEDLE 2: Knit.

NEEDLE 3: K1, SSK, knit to end—2 sts dec each dec rnd.

NEXT RND: Knit even.

Work these 2 rnds until 60 sts rem.

FOOT

Cont in St st on 60 sts until foot measures 1¾" (4cm) less than desired length.

BEGIN TOE SHAPING: DEC RND

NEEDLE 1: Knit to last 3 sts, k2tog, k1.

NEEDLE 2: K1, SSK, knit to last 3 sts, k2tog, k1.

NEEDLE 3: K1, SSK, knit to end—4 sts dec each dec rnd.

NEXT RND: Knit even.

Work these 2 rnds until 28 sts rem, then rep dec rnd every rnd until 12 sts rem.

Divide sts onto 2 needles. Graft tog using Kitchener st. See the Glossary, page 141, for instructions on grafting with Kitchener st.

Weave in all ends.

CHART 1

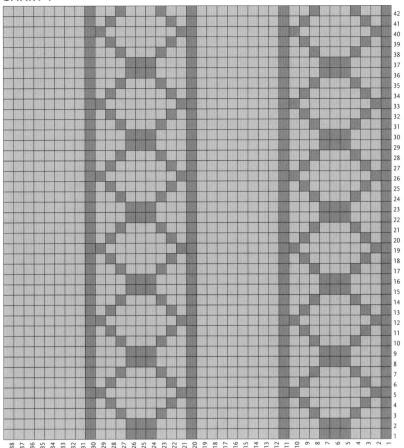

CHART 2

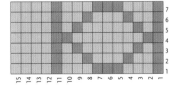

CHART 3

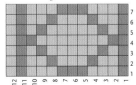

KEY ☐ knit

☐ purl

Cuddle Bear

WHAT DAUGHTER WOULDN'T LOVE TO RECEIVE A CUDDLY BEAR FROM HER MOTHER?
I made him nice and big, so no matter your daughter's age, she can give him a
good squeeze. Knit out of Rowan Kid Classic in the appropriately named yarn
color "Bear," he is soft with a nice fuzzy halo. Dress him up with a colorful scarf,
or knit the romper suit my bear wears.

FINISHED MEASUREMENTS
approx 22" (56cm) tall

YARN
3 skeins Rowan Kid Classic (lambswool/mohair/nylon
blend, 50 g, 153 yds [140m]) for bear
> color #817 Bear

1 skein Rowan Kid Classic each in the foll colors for romper suit
> color #853 Spruce (MC)
> color #845 Battle (CC)

NEEDLES AND NOTIONS
16" (41cm) and 24" (61cm) size US 7 (4.5mm) circular needles

size US 7 (4.5mm) double-pointed needles

16" (41cm) size US 8 (5.0mm) circular needle (for romper suit)

waste yarn for provisional cast on

yarn needle

sew-on eyes, approx ⅝" to ¾" (2cm) in diameter

black worsted or bulky weight scrap yarn for nose

polyester fiberfill

GAUGE
18 sts x 24 rows = 4" (10cm) in St st with size US 7 (4.5mm) needles

TECHNIQUES

SHORT ROW SHAPING

(RS) WRAP AND TURN (W&T): Wyif, sl 1 st from the left needle to the right. Move the yarn to the back, sl st back to the left needle, turn work. 1 st has been wrapped.

(WS) WRAP AND TURN (W&T): Wyib, sl 1 st from the left needle to the right. Move the yarn to the front, sl st back to the left needle, turn work. 1 st has been wrapped.

⁓ NOTE ⁓
Whenever you come to a wrap, work the wrap tog with the st it wraps. To pick up a wrap and its st, slide the tip of the right needle into the wrap from the front of the work and place the wrap on the left needle alongside the st it wraps. Knit the 2 loops tog as one st tbl.

K2TOG (KNIT 2 TOGETHER): Dec 1 st by knitting 2 sts tog.

P2TOG (PURL 2 TOGETHER): Dec 1 st by purling 2 sts tog.

P3TOG (PURL 3 TOGETHER): Dec 2 sts by purling 3 sts tog.

M1 (MAKE 1): Inc 1 st by picking up, from front to back, the bar between the next st and the st just knit and placing it on the left needle. Knit into the back of the picked-up st.

SSK (SLIP, SLIP, KNIT): Dec 1 st by slipping 2 sts knitwise one at a time from the left needle to the right needle. Insert the tip of the left needle into the front of both sts and knit the 2 sts tog.

Bear

MUZZLE
With size US 7 (4.5mm) needles and waste yarn, CO 13 sts using a provisional cast on.

⁓ NOTE ⁓
To work a provisional cast on, crochet a chain with scrap yarn several chains longer than the number of sts you will be casting on. Cut yarn and tie off crochet chain. Leaving a tail, knit the number of cast-on sts indicated in the patt through the back loops of the crochet chain.

Work in St st for 2 rows. Cut waste yarn.

With MC, knit 1 row—13 sts.

SECTION 1

ROW 1: P3, w&t.

ROW 2 AND ALL EVEN-NUMBERED ROWS: Knit to end.

ROW 3: P5, w&t.

ROW 5: P7, w&t.

ROW 7: P9, w&t.

ROW 9: P11, w&t.

ROW 11: P13.

ROWS 12–16: Work in St st.

ROW 17: P11, w&t.

ROW 19: P9, w&t.

ROW 21: P7, w&t.

ROW 23: P5, w&t.

ROW 25: P3, w&t.

ROWS 26–28: Work in St st.

SECTION 2

ROW 1: P5, w&t.

ROW 2 AND ALL EVEN-NUMBERED ROWS: Knit to end.

ROW 3: P9, w&t.

ROW 5: P13.

ROWS 6–8: Work in St st.

ROW 9: P9, w&t.

ROW 11: P5, w&t.

ROWS 12–14: Work in St st.

Rep Rows 1–28 of section 1.

Cut yarn, leaving a long tail for grafting.

Remove waste yarn from cast-on edge and place 13 sts on a needle. Graft sts from 2 needles tog using Kitchener st. Do not sew up center hole. Sts will be picked up later with black yarn to knit nose.

⁓ NOTE ⁓
To graft with Kitchener st, line up both sets of live sts on 2 separate needles with the tips facing the same direction. Thread a yarn needle onto the tail of the back piece. Begin by performing the foll steps once: Bring the needle through the first st on the needle closest to you as if to purl, leaving the st on the needle. Then insert the needle through the first st on the back needle as if to knit, leaving the st on the needle. Now you are ready to graft. * Bring the needle through the first st on the front needle as if to knit, slipping the st off the needle. Bring the needle through the next st on the front needle as if to purl, leaving the st on the needle. Then bring the needle through the first st on the back needle as if to purl, sliding the st off the needle. Bring the needle through the next st on the back needle as if to knit, leaving the st on the needle. Rep from * until all sts are grafted tog. Approx every 2" (5cm), tighten up the sts, starting at the beg of the join. Slip the tip of the yarn needle under each leg of each Kitchener st and pull up gently until the tension is correct. Rep across the entire row of grafted sts. It may help you to say to yourself, "Knit, purl – purl, knit" as you go.

HEAD

Place grafted row at bottom center of muzzle.

ROW 1: With RS facing, pick up and knit 44 sts along top two-thirds of muzzle.

ROW 2 (WS): Purl across.

ROWS 3–6: Cont in St st, ending with a WS row.

ROW 7 (DEC ROW): * K9, k2tog; rep from * to end—40 sts.

ROWS 8–12: Work even in St st.

ROW 13 (DEC ROW): * K8, k2tog; rep from * to end—36 sts.

ROWS 14–18: Work even in St st.

ROW 19 (DEC ROW): * K7, k2tog; rep from * to end—32 sts.

ROWS 20–24: Work even in St st.

ROW 25 (DEC ROW): * K6, k2tog; rep from * to end—28 sts.

ROW 26: Purl even.

ROWS 27–35: Cont dec in this manner EOR, having 1 less st between dec until Row 35 which will be: * K1, k2tog; rep from * to end—8 sts.

ROW 36: P2tog across row—4 sts.

Break yarn, pull tight through rem sts.

BOTTOM OF HEAD

ROW 1: With RS facing, using 24" (61cm) size US 7 circular needle, and starting at center back where you just ended off, pick up and knit 100 sts evenly spaced around bottom of head, including muzzle. Do not join.

ROWS 2–4: Work back and forth in St st, ending with a WS row.

ROW 5: * K8, k2tog; rep from * to end of row—90 sts.

ROW 6: Purl even.

ROW 7: * K7, k2tog; rep from * to end of row—80 sts.

ROW 8: Purl even.

ROWS 9–19: Cont dec in this manner EOR, having 1 less st between dec until Row 19, which will be: * K1, k2tog; rep from * to end—20 sts.

ROW 20: Purl even.

BODY

ROW 1: * K1, m1; rep from * to last st, k1—39 sts.

ROW 2: Purl.

ROW 3: * K2, m1; rep from * to last st, k1—58 sts.

ROW 4: Purl.

ROW 5: * K3, m1; rep from * to last st, k1—77 sts.

ROWS 6–28: Work in St st for 23 rows, ending with a WS row.

ROW 29: * K4, m1; rep from * to last st, k1—96 sts.

ROWS 30–32: Work 3 rows in St st.

ROW 33: * K5, m1; rep from * to last st, k1—115 sts.

Cont straight until body measures 10" (25cm), or desired length.

BOTTOM OF BODY

ROW 1 (DEC ROW): * K2, k2tog; rep from * to last 3 sts, ending k1, k2tog—86 sts.

ROW 2: Purl.

ROW 3 (DEC ROW): * K1, k2tog; rep from * to last 2 sts, ending k2—58 sts.

ROW 4: Purl.

LEGS (MAKE 2)

BO 7, k15 for leg, BO 14, k15 for Leg, BO 7. Break off yarn.

Place 1 leg on a st holder, attach yarn to other leg. Divide sts evenly over 3 DPNs. Join for working in the rnd.

RND 1: With RS facing, knit—15 sts.

RND 2 (INC RND): * K1, m1; rep from * to end of rnd—30 sts.

RND 3: Knit even.

RND 4 (INC RND): * K7, m1; rep from * to last 2 sts, k2—34 sts.

Cont working even in St st until leg measures 8" (20cm).

DEC RND: * K2tog; rep from * to end of rnd—17 sts.

Knit 1 rnd even.

DEC RND: * K2tog; rep from * to last st, k1—9 sts.

Break yarn, pull tight through rem sts.

Rep for other leg.

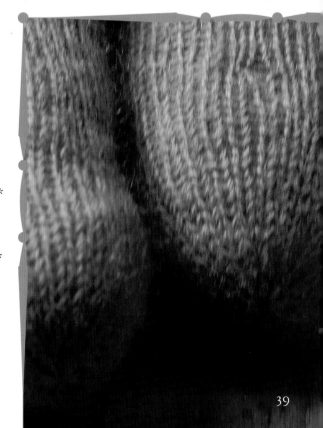

ARMS (MAKE 2)

With size US 7 (4.5mm) DPNs, CO 8 sts. Join for working in the rnd.

RND 1: Knit—8 sts.

RND 2: * K1, m1; rep from * to end of rnd—16 sts.

RND 3: Knit.

RND 4: * K1, m1; rep from * to end of rnd—32 sts.

Cont working even in St st for 5" (13cm).

DEC RND: * K2tog; rep from * to end of rnd—16 sts.

Stuff arm with polyester fiberfill.

Knit 1 rnd even.

DEC RND: * K2tog; rep from * to end of rnd—8 sts.

Break yarn, pull tight through rem sts.

EARS (MAKE 4 PIECES)

CO 8 sts.

ROW 1 (RS): Knit.

ROW 2 (WS): P2, w&t.

ROW 3: Knit to end.

ROW 4: P4, w&t.

ROW 5: Knit to end.

ROW 6: P6, w&t.

ROW 7: Knit to end.

ROW 8: P8.

ROW 9: Knit to last st, m1, k1—9 sts.

ROW 10: Purl.

ROW 11: Knit to last st, m1, k1—10 sts.

ROW 12: P8, w&t.

ROW 13: Knit to last st, m1, k1—11 sts.

ROW 14: P7, w&t.

ROW 15: Knit to last st, m1, k1—12 sts.

ROW 16: P9, w&t.

ROW 17: Knit to last st, m1, k1—13 sts.

ROW 18: Purl to end.

ROW 19: Knit to last st, m1, k1—14 sts.

ROW 20: P8, w&t.

ROW 21: Knit to end.

ROW 22: P10, w&t.

ROW 23: Knit to end.

ROW 24: P12, w&t.

ROW 25: Knit to end.

ROW 26: P14.

ROW 27: Knit 1 row.

ROW 28: P12, w&t.

ROW 29: Knit to end.

ROW 30: P10, w&t.

ROW 31: Knit to end.

ROW 32: P8, w&t.

ROW 33: Knit to end.

ROW 34: Purl to end.

ROW 35: Knit to last 3 sts, k2tog, k1—13 sts.

ROW 36: P7, w&t.

ROW 37: Knit to last 3 sts, k2tog, k1—12 sts.

ROW 38: P8, w&t.

ROW 39: Knit to last 3 sts, k2tog, k1—11 sts.

ROW 40: P9, w&t.

ROW 41: Knit to last 3 sts, k2tog, k1—10 sts.

ROW 42: Purl to end.

ROW 43: Knit to last 3 sts, k2tog, k1—9 sts.

ROW 44: Purl.

ROW 45: Knit to last 3 sts, k2tog, k1—8 sts.

ROW 46: P6, w&t.

ROW 47: Knit to end.

ROW 48: P4, w&t.

ROW 49: Knit to end.

ROW 50: P2, w&t.

ROW 51: Knit to end.

ROW 52: Purl to end.

ROW 53: Knit to end.

BO all sts.

ASSEMBLE EARS

Hold the 2 ears tog with WS facing and seam them tog with mattress st, working all around each ear. See the Glossary, page 141, for instructions on working in mattress st.

Position each ear as in photo, slightly curved forward. Secure in place along front and back of each ear with mattress st.

FINISHING

NOSE

ROW 1: With scrap black yarn and US size 7 (4.5 mm) needles and RS facing, pick up and knit 13 sts along top of nose opening in muzzle—13 sts.

ROW 2: Purl 1 row.

ROW 3: K1, SSK, knit to last 3 sts, k2tog, k1—11 sts.

ROW 4: P1, p2tog, purl to last 3 sts, p2tog, p1—9 sts.

ROWS 5–6: Rep Rows 3–4 once—5 sts rem.

ROW 7: SSK, k1, k2tog—3 sts.

ROW 8: P3tog—1 st.

Break yarn, leaving a tail for sewing. Pull tight through rem st. Stitch nose into place.

Attach arms at sides. Finish stuffing and sew bear tog between legs and up center back seam using mattress st. Attach eyes. Weave in all loose ends.

If you find your bear's head is a bit too floppy, tip his head forward a bit and stitch it in place just above and below the neck.

Romper Suit

LEGS (MAKE 2)
With size US 7 (4.5mm) needles and MC, CO 54 sts. Work back and forth in k1, p1 ribbing for 4 rows. Switch to size US 8 (5.0mm) needles. Work in St st for 8 rows. Place on a holder.

BODY
Place sts from both Legs on size US 8 (5.0mm) 16" (41cm) circular needle.

RND 1: With MC, knit across 54 sts of 1 Leg, and then 54 sts of other leg, being careful not to twist sts where legs join—108 sts total. Pm at beg of rnd (center back).

RNDS 2–15: With MC work in St st—108 sts.

RND 16: Work in CC.

RND 17: Work in MC.

RNDS 18–21: Rep Rnds 16–17 twice more.

RND 22: Work in CC.

RNDS 23–25: Work in MC.

RND 26: Work in CC.

RND 27: Work in MC.

RNDS 28–29: Rep Rnds 26–27 once more.

RNDS 30–41: Work in CC.

RND 42: Work in MC.

RND 43: Work in CC.

RNDS 44–45: Rep Rnds 42–43 once more.

RNDS 46–48: Work in MC. End MC. Switch to CC and work as foll:

RND 49: K27, pm, k54, pm, k27.

RND 50 (DEC RND): Knit to 3 sts before marker, k2tog, k1, sm, k1, SSK, knit to 3 sts before marker, k2tog, k1, sm, k1, SSK, knit to end of rnd—104 sts.

RND 51: Knit even.

RNDS 52–59: Rep Rnds 50–51 4 times more—88 sts rem.

Bind off for neck opening and armholes:

NEXT ROW: BO 8 sts, * k6 sts and place on a holder, BO 16 sts; rep from * twice more; k6 sts and place on a holder, BO 8 sts.

SHOULDER STRAPS
For each 6 sts on holders, work as foll (4 straps):

With RS facing, place 6 sts on size US 8 (5.0mm) needle and join CC yarn. Work in St st for 10 rows. BO.

Join front and back straps at shoulder seam.

NECK BAND
With size US 7 (4.5mm) DPNs or 16" (41cm) circular needle and CC, pick up and knit an even number of sts evenly spaced around the neck opening. Join for working in the rnd, pm at beg of rnd. Work in k1, p1 ribbing for 4 rnds. BO in rib.

ARM BANDS
With size US 7 (4.5mm) DPNs and MC, pick up and knit an even number of sts evenly spaced around each armhole. Join for working in the rnd, pm at beg of rnd. Work in k1, p1 ribbing for 4 rnds. BO in rib.

Weave in all ends.

41

Cap-Sleeved Eyelet Top

Do you hesitate to knit your daughter a sweater for fear she won't like it? Well, look no further than this cap-sleeved top, knit with 100 percent alpaca yarn. Featuring a scoop neck, a defined waist and a pretty eyelet pattern, this top will flatter her and keep her warm.

CHART

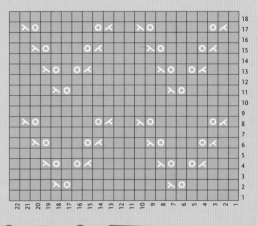

KEY

⊠ **SSK:** On RS SSK; on WS, sl 1, p1, psso

⊡ **YO:** Yarn over

⊠ **WORK 2 TOG:** On RS, k2tog; on WS, p2tog

SIZES
S (M, L)

To fit bust sizes 32–34 (34–36, 36–38)" (81–86 [86–91, 91–97]cm)

FINISHED MEASUREMENTS
Bust measurement: 32 (34, 36)" (81 [86, 91]cm), unstretched

ෞ NOTE ෞ
This is a close-fitting, stretchy garment. For a closer fit, select the size with the bust measurement you want on the high end of the range. For a looser fitting top, select the size with the bust measurement you want on the low end of the range. Top shown in size Medium.

YARN
7 skeins Classic Elite Inca Alpaca (100% alpaca, 50 g, 109 yds [100m])
   color # 1116 Natural

NEEDLES AND NOTIONS
24" (61cm) size US 6 (4.0mm) circular needle

24" (61cm) US size 7 (4.5mm) circular needle

markers

yarn needle

GAUGE
20 sts x 28 rows = 4" (10cm) in St st with larger needles

TECHNIQUES
K2TOG (KNIT 2 TOGETHER): Dec 1 st by knitting 2 sts tog.

P2TOG (PURL 2 TOGETHER): Dec 1 st by purling 2 sts tog.

WORK 2 TOG (KNIT OR PURL 2 TOGETHER): Dec 1 st by knitting or purling 2 sts tog as one, in keeping with est patt.

M1 (MAKE 1): Inc 1 st by picking up, from front to back, the bar between the next st and the st just knit and placing it on the left needle. Knit into the back of the picked-up st.

SSK (SLIP, SLIP, KNIT): Dec 1 st by slipping 2 sts knitwise one at a time from the left needle to the right needle. Insert the tip of the left needle into the front of both sts and knit the 2 sts tog.

YO (YARN OVER): Wrap working yarn around needle clockwise, and knit the next st as usual. This operation creates an eyelet hole in the knitting and inc 1 st.

PSSO (PASS SLIPPED ST OVER): Insert the tip of the left needle into the slipped st(s) on the right needle and slide it onto the left needle, bringing it over any knitted st(s) to dec.

Top

BODY

With size US 6 (4.0mm) circular needle, CO 165 (175, 185) sts. Pm and join for working in the rnd, taking care not to twist sts. Work in k2, p3 ribbing for 3½ (3½, 4)" (9 [9, 10]cm).

NEXT RND: Switch to size US 7 (4.5 mm) circular needle, sm, k8 (11, 13), pm, work Row 1 of chart for 66 sts for front, pm, k8 (11, 13), pm, k8 (11, 13), pm, work Row 1 of chart for 66 sts for back, pm, k7 (10, 12), ending rnd with: Size S: (k2tog); Size M: (m1); Size L: (k2tog)—164 (176, 184) sts.

NEXT RND: K8 (11, 13), sm, work Row 2 of chart across front center 66 sts, sm, k8 (11, 13), sm, k8 (11, 13), work Row 2 of chart across center back 66 sts, sm, k8 (11, 13).

Cont to work front and back lace panels from chart, reading each row of chart from right to left for circular knitting.

DEC RND: K1, k2tog, knit to marker, sm, work center front sts, sm, knit to 3 sts before marker, k2tog, k1, sm, k1, k2tog, knit to marker, sm, work center back sts, sm, knit to 3 sts before marker, k2tog, k1—160 (172, 180) sts.

Work this dec rnd every 6th row 5 times more, keeping side sts in St st and cont to work chart across center front and back panels—140 (152, 160) sts.

Work even in est patt, ending with row 9 of fourth chart rep.

NEXT ROW (SIZES S AND L ONLY): Work 1 rnd even in St st— 140 (---, 160) sts.

SIZE M ONLY: K74, k2tog, k74, k2tog—150 sts.

WAIST

இ **NOTE** இ
Keep markers in place.

With size US 6 (4.0mm) circular needle, work in k2, p3 ribbing for 2½ (2½, 3)" (6 [6, 8]cm), retaining markers.

Change to size US 7 (4.5mm) circular needle.

SIZES S AND L ONLY: Work 1 rnd even in St st—140 (---, 160) sts.

SIZE M ONLY: K75, m1, k75, m1—152 sts.

INC RND: K1, m1, knit to marker, sm, work chart starting with Row 1 across front center panel, sm, knit to 1 st before marker, m1, k1, sm, k1, m1, knit to marker, work chart across back center panel, sm, knit to 1 st before marker, m1, k1—144 (156, 164) sts.

Work this inc rnd every 6th row 5 times more—164 (176, 184) sts.

Cont as est until piece measures 18 (18, 19)" (46 [46, 48]cm), or desired length, ending with Row 8 of chart.

FRONT

BEGIN ARMHOLE SHAPING

BO 5 (5, 6), knit to marker, work Row 9 of chart across front center panel, sm, knit to marker, turn. Place all 82 (88, 92) back sts on a holder and work back and forth on the front—77 (83, 86) sts.

இ **NOTE** இ
Cont to work lace patt as est to end of shoulder bind off.

BO 5 (5, 6), purl to end, removing all markers—72 (78, 80) sts.

ARMHOLE DEC: K1, SSK, work 20 (23, 24) sts, BO center 26 sts, work to last 3 sts, k2tog, k1.

Place left shoulder sts on a holder.

WORK RIGHT SHOULDER

(WS) Purl to neck edge—22 (25, 26) sts.

Begin neck shaping and cont armhole shaping:

NECK DEC (RS): K1, SSK, work to 3 sts before armhole edge, k2tog, k1—20 (23, 24) sts.

Rep neck dec EOR 4 times more, AND AT THE SAME TIME, rep armhole dec EOR 4 (4, 5) times more, then every 4th row once—11 (14, 14) sts.

Work even in patt until armhole measures 7¼ (7½, 8)" (18 [19, 20]cm), ending with a RS row.

BEGIN SHOULDER SHAPING

ROW 1 (WS): BO 4 (5, 5) sts, purl to end—7 (9, 9) sts.

ROW 2 (RS): Knit across.

ROW 3: BO 4 (5, 5) sts, purl to end—3 (4, 4) sts.

ROW 4: BO rem 3 (4, 4) sts.

LEFT SHOULDER

With WS facing, attach yarn and purl to end—22 (25, 26) sts.

Begin neck shaping and cont armhole shaping:

(RS) K1, SSK, work to last 3 sts at neck edge, k2tog, k1—20 (23, 24) sts.

Rep neck edge dec EOR 4 times more, AND AT THE SAME TIME, rep armhole dec EOR 4 (4, 5) times more, then every 4th row once—11 (14, 14) sts.

Work even in patt until armhole measures 7¼ (7½, 8)" (18 [19, 20]cm), ending with a WS row.

BEGIN SHOULDER SHAPING

ROW 1 (RS): BO 4 (5, 5) sts, work to end—7 (9, 9) sts.

ROW 2: Purl across.

ROW 3: BO 4 (5, 5) sts, work to end—3 (4, 4) sts.

ROW 4: BO rem 3 (4, 4) sts.

BACK

Place 82 (88, 92) sts from holder onto size US 7 (4.5mm) circular needle and attach yarn, with RS facing, removing all markers.

BO 5 (5, 6) sts at the beg of the next 2 rows, maintaining chart pattern as est for remainder of back—72 (78, 80) sts.

DEC ROW: K1, SSK, work to last 3 sts, k2tog, k1—70 (76, 78) sts.

Rep dec row EOR 5 (5, 6) times more, then every 4th row once—58 (64, 64) sts.

Work even in est patt until armhole measures 7 (7¼, 7¾)" (18 [18, 20]cm).

BEGIN NECK AND SHOULDER SHAPING
Work 22 (25, 25) sts, BO center 14 sts, work to end. Place left shoulder sts on a holder.

WORK RIGHT SHOULDER

ROW 1 (WS): Purl to neck edge—22 (25, 25) sts.

ROW 2: BO 6 sts at neck edge, work to end—16 (19, 19) sts.

ROW 3: BO 4 (5, 5) sts at armhole edge, purl to end—12 (14, 14) sts.

ROW 4: BO 5 sts at neck edge, work to end—7 (9, 9) sts.

ROW 5: BO 4 (5, 5) sts, purl to end—3 (4, 4) sts.

ROW 6: BO rem 3 (4, 4) sts.

LEFT SHOULDER

ROW 1: With WS facing, attach yarn and purl to end—22 (25, 25) sts.

ROW 2 (RS): Work to end.

ROW 3 (WS): BO 6 sts at neck edge, purl to end—16 (19, 19) sts.

ROW 4: BO 4 (5, 5) sts at armhole edge, work to end—12 (14, 14) sts.

ROW 5: BO 5 sts at neck edge, purl to end—7 (9, 9) sts.

ROW 6: BO 4 (5, 5) sts at armhole edge, work to end—3 (4, 4) sts.

ROW 7: BO rem 3 (4, 4) sts.

SLEEVES (MAKE 2)
With size US 6 (4.0mm) circular needle, CO 62 (62, 64) sts. Work back and forth in k1, p1 ribbing for 1½ (1½, 2)" (4 [5, 5]cm).

With size US 7 (4.5 mm) circular needle, work in St st for 2 rows, ending with a WS row.

∞ NOTE ∞
Remainder of sleeve is worked in St st.

BEGIN CAP SHAPING
BO 5 (5, 6) sts at the beg of the next 2 rows—52 sts.

BO 2 sts at the beg of the next 4 rows—44 sts.

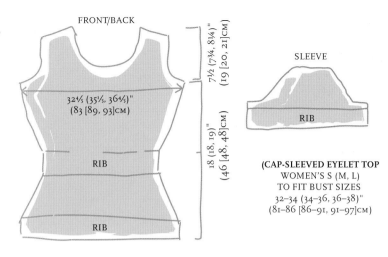

FRONT/BACK

32½ (35½, 36½)" (83 [89, 93]cm)

RIB

RIB

7½ (7¾, 8¼)" (19 [20, 21]cm)

18 (18, 19)" (46 [48, 48]cm)

SLEEVE

RIB

(CAP-SLEEVED EYELET TOP WOMEN'S S (M, L) TO FIT BUST SIZES 32–34 (34–36, 36–38)" (81–86 [86–91, 91–97]cm)

DEC ROW: K1, SSK, knit to last 3 sts, k2tog, k1—42 sts.

Rep this row EOR 9 times more—24 sts.

BO 4 sts at the beg of the next 2 rows—16 sts.

BO rem 16 sts.

FINISHING
Block all pieces for easier assembly. Using mattress st, sew shoulder seams. Sew up sleeve seam. Ease sleeves into armholes and sew into place. See the Glossary, page 141, for instructions on working in mattress st.

NECK BAND
Pick up an even number of sts, evenly spaced, around neck with size US 6 (4.0mm) circular needle. Work in k1, p1 ribbing for 1" (3cm). BO loosely.

Weave in all ends.

45

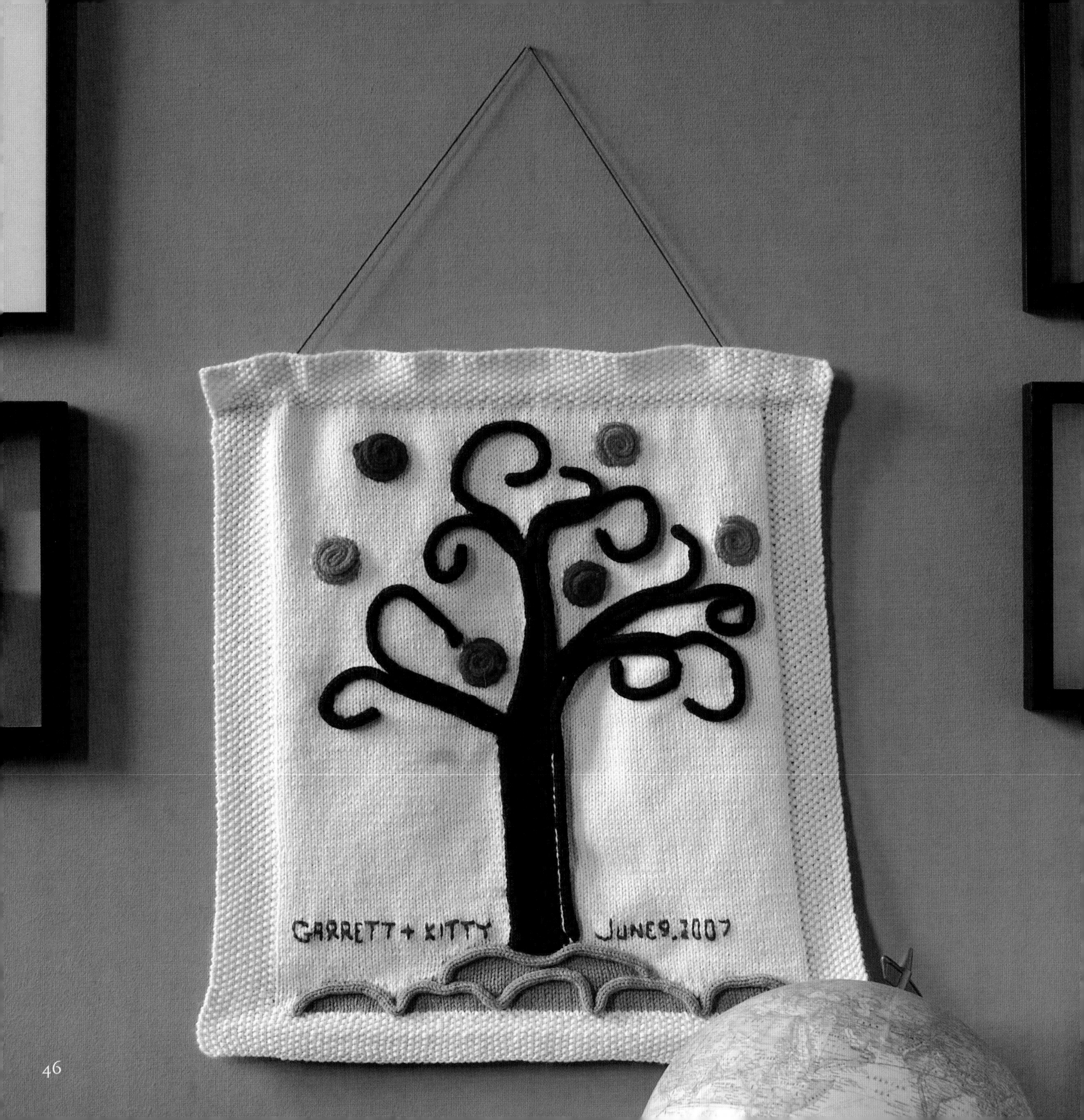
GARRETT + KITTY
JUNE 9, 2007

Tree of Love Wall Hanging

ARE YOU LOOKING FOR JUST THE RIGHT GIFT TO MARK A MILESTONE IN YOUR DAUGHTER'S LIFE? This wall hanging could be just the thing. I created the one shown as a wedding gift for my cousin, with the idea that they can add to it as their family grows. I used an I-cord maker called the Embellish-Knit!, an affordable gadget available at various craft supply stores, to assist in the many feet of I-cord necessary for this project. You may use this wall hanging as a guide, or you may choose to free-form your I-cords in a different fashion. Have fun with it!

FINISHED MEASUREMENTS
21" x 21" (53cm x 53cm)

YARN
2 skeins Cascade 220 (100% Peruvian Highland wool, 100 g, 220 yds [201m])
   color # 8010 White (MC)

1 skein Cascade 220 in each of the foll colors:
   color #7822 Tree (CC1)
   color #8914 Green (CC2)
   color #7824 Orange (CC3)
   color #2427 Burgundy (CC4)

NEEDLES AND NOTIONS
size US 7 (4.5mm) straight or circular needles

size US 7 (4.5mm) double-pointed needles or Embellish-Knit! I-cord maker

(2) 20" (51cm) dowel rods, ½" (1cm) in diameter

yarn needle

GAUGE
20 sts x 28 rows = 4" (10cm) in St st

ANOTHER GIFT IDEA
While this pattern is featured in the Daughters chapter, it could be made to celebrate other loved ones as well. This would be an excellent platform for a family tree to be given to parents or grandparents, with all the appropriate names embroidered onto it. It could also be an excellent baby shower gift.

Wall Hanging

With MC, CO 101 sts.

BEGIN SEED ST BORDER

ROW 1: K1, * p1, k1; rep from * to end of row.

ROWS 2–14: Rep Row 1.

NEXT ROW (RS): Work 10 sts as est in seed st (for right-side border), pm, work 81 sts of Row 1 of chart in St st, beg with a RS (knit) row, pm, work last 10 sts as est in seed st (for left-side border). Foll chart from right to left for RS rows and from left to right for WS rows. Work color areas of chart using intarsia technique and twisting the 2 colors of yarn at each join to prevent holes. See the Glossary, page 139, for instructions on working in intarsia.

Cont to foll chart until tree is completed and entire piece measures approx 19" (48cm) from cast-on edge.

TOP BORDER: Work 14 rows in est seed st on all sts for border. Bind off loosely in pattern.

TREE I-CORD

Make the foll lengths of I-cord using CC1: 14" (36cm), 16" (41cm), 17" (43cm), 19" (48cm), 20" (51cm), 21" (53cm).

℘ NOTE ℘

To make I-cord, cast on 3 sts to a DPN. Knit 1 row. Slide sts to opposite end of needle. * Pulling yarn across back, knit 1 row. Slide sts to opposite end of needle. Rep from *, creating I-cord. When you reach desired length, break yarn, pull tight through all sts. Or use an I-cord maker.

Attach I-cord to wall hanging, foll tree trunk and branches and coiling into pictured shapes. To attach the I-cord to the wall hanging, thread a yarn needle with yarn that matches the I-cord to be sewn. Work mattress st up and down each side of the I-cord, pulling tight to keep the seam invisible. See the Glossary, page 141, for instructions on working in mattress st.

GRASS I-CORD

Make the foll lengths of I-cord using CC2: 20" (51cm) and 7½" (19cm). Attach the I-cord as per picture.

FRUIT I-CORD

Make 7 8" (20cm) lengths of I-cord out of CC3 and CC4. Coil each I-cord into a fruit shape, and then whip stitch each fruit shape in place across the back of the fruit. Attach the fruit to the backdrop using mattress st all the way around, pulling yarn tight to keep the seam invisible.

FINISHING

With WS facing, place dowels ½" (1cm) from top and bottom of wall hanging. Whip stitch each dowel rod in place down the entire length of each dowel. Hang the piece with yarn, string or ribbon tied to each end of the top dowel.

QUICK FIX

The most time-consuming part of this project is knitting up the backdrop. (If you have the Embellish-Knit! to help you crank out the I-cord, that part will take no time at all.) To save time, you might purchase a pillow and design a tree to stitch onto it. Or finish the edges of heavy canvas to use as the backdrop for the wall hanging. True, there is a bit of color work in the original backdrop, but you will be fine without it—you can always "color in" with extra I-cord. If you decide to attach I-cord onto canvas, you will want to use a sewing needle and thread.

KEY

Knit on RS, purl on WS	☐
CC1	▨
CC2	▨
CC3	☐
CC4	▨

Sisters

I DESIGNED THE PROJECTS IN THIS CHAPTER WITH
MY YOUNGER SISTER, THERESA, IN MIND. If I had to
choose one word to describe her, it would be vibrant.
Her bright and energetic personality inspired the color
palettes in this chapter. Reds, purples, greens and more...
she would have a ball running around town or decorating
her home with these projects. I hope something in this
chapter catches your eye as you think about your own
sister. Would she like a L-O-N-G, multi-directional scarf
(see page 52), or a sweet A-line *Tiered Skirt* (see page 66)?
Maybe she'd like *Embroidered Flower Socks* (see page 56)
or a warm *Bright Stripes Throw* (see page 64). How about
a soft *Pinwheel Pillow* in vibrant shades (see page 60)?

Do you notice a certain color always showing up in
your sister's wardrobe or home? Feel free to work with
what you know she loves. When deciding what to create,
what do you think she would especially enjoy? Does she
always have a scarf wrapped around her neck? Is she a
skirt girl? When she curls up to watch a movie
or read a book, is it usually with a cozy blanket?

I had such fun creating each and every one of
these projects. Enjoy!

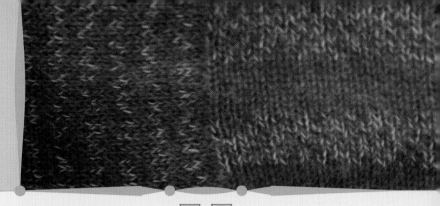

Multi-Directional Scarf and Hat

SOMETIMES YOU WANT TO KNIT A NICE LONG SCARF. When the mood strikes you, try this one out. Knit in five sections, you won't even realize how much knitting has grown from your needles until it's done and you say, "Wow!" And your sister will say "wow," too, when you pair it with the coordinating hat, featuring some multi-directional knitting of its own.

FINISHED SIZES
Pattern given is for a women's medium.

See pattern for how to make hat taller.

FINISHED MEASUREMENTS
Scarf: 10" x 69" (25cm x 175cm)
Hat: 19" (48cm) around x 6" (15cm) tall

YARN
4 skeins Classic Elite Inca (100% alpaca, 50 g, 109 yds [100m])
   color #1135 Cala Cala Moss (MC)

3 skeins Classic Elite Inca Marl (100% alpaca, 50 g, 109 yds [100m])
   color #1171 Shamrock (CC)

ANOTHER GIFT IDEA: VARIATION SCARF
2 skeins Classic Elite Inca in each of the foll colors:
   color #1198 Persimmon (A)
   color #1134 Whisper (B)
   color #1151 Tulip (C)

1 skein Classic Elite
   color #1184 Pomegranate (D)

Instructions for the variation given in parentheses.

NEEDLES
16" (41cm) size US 6 (4.0mm) circular needle

16" (41cm) size US 7 (4.5mm) circular needle

1 set of 5 size US 7 (4.5mm) double-pointed needles

GAUGE
20 sts x 28 rows = 4" (10cm) in St st using size 7 (4.5mm) needles

TECHNIQUES
K2TOG (KNIT 2 TOGETHER): Dec 1 st by knitting 2 sts tog.

Hat

With size US 6 (4.0mm) circular needle and MC, CO 104 sts. Join for working in the rnd, pm to mark beg of rnd. Work in k1, p1 rib for 8 rnds.

◌ɔ NOTE ɔ◌
If you usually wear a larger hat size, add more rnds of ribbing.

Switch to size US 7 (4.5mm) circular needle and CC. Work in St st for 2 rnds.

NEXT RND: Remove marker, BO 15 sts, work to end of rnd.

Now work back and forth on 89 sts.

Work 3 more rows with CC.

SWITCH TO MC: Work in St st for 6 rows.

SWITCH TO CC: Work in St st for 6 rows.

SWITCH TO MC: Work in St st for 3 rows, ending with a RS row.

PM, CO 15 sts at beg of next row, knit to end of rnd. Work 2 more rnds in MC.

SWITCH TO CC: Work in St st for 6 rnds.

BEGIN SHAPING CROWN
Switch to MC.

DEC RND: * K11, k2tog; rep from * to end of rnd—96 sts.

NEXT RND: Knit.

NEXT RND: Switch to MC. * K2, k2tog; rep from * to end of rnd—72 sts.

NEXT RND: Knit.

Change to size 7 (4.5mm) DPNs when necessary.

NEXT RND: Switch to CC. * K1, k2tog; rep from * to end of rnd—48 sts.

NEXT RND: Knit.

NEXT RND: Switch to MC. K2tog around—24sts.

Break yarn, leaving a tail. Weave through rem sts and pull tight. Weave in all ends.

PATCH
With MC, pick up 14 sts along 1 vertical edge of gap in hat. Work 2 rows. Switch to CC, work 2 rows. Cont in this manner, alt colors every 2 rows, until 10 rows are completed. Place sts on holder. With CC, pick up 14 sts along the other vertical edge of gap in hat. Work 2 rows. Switch to MC, work 2 rows. Cont in this manner, alt colors every 2 rows until 9 rows are completed.

Leave sts on needle. Using long CC yarn tail, graft 14 sts from needle with 14 sts from holder using Kitchener stitch. Stitch patch at top and bottom to hat.

Weave in all ends.

◌ɔ NOTE ɔ◌
To graft with Kitchener st, line up both sets of live sts on 2 separate needles with the tips facing the same direction. Thread a yarn needle onto the tail of the back piece. Begin by performing the foll steps once: Bring the needle through the first st on the needle closest to you as if to purl, leaving the st on the needle. Then insert the needle through the first st on the back needle as if to knit, leaving the st on the needle. Now you are ready to graft. * Bring the needle through the first st on the front needle as if to knit, slipping the st off the needle. Bring the needle through the next st on the front needle as if to purl, leaving the st on the needle. Then bring the needle through the first st on the back needle as if to purl, sliding the st off the needle. Bring the needle through the next st on the back needle as if to knit, leaving the st on the needle. Rep from * until all sts are grafted tog. Approx every 2" (5cm), tighten up the sts, starting at the beg of the join. Slip the tip of the yarn needle under each leg of each Kitchener st and pull up gently until the tension is correct. Rep across the entire row of grafted sts. It may help you to say to yourself, "Knit, purl – purl, knit" as you go.

Scarf

The middle section of the scarf will be worked first. The 2 end sections are knit last and sewn perpendicular to the middle section.

MIDDLE SECTION

With size US 7 (4.5mm) circular needle and MC, loosely cast on 50 sts.

Work 84 rows in St st in the foll patt:

COLOR PATTERN 1:

ROWS 1–2: MC (C).

ROWS 3–4: CC (D).

Rep Rows 1–4 20 times more.

Cont in St st in the foll patt:

COLOR PATTERN 2:

ROWS 1–10: MC (A).

ROWS 11–18: CC (B).

ROWS 19–26: MC (A).

Note: For variation scarf, foll patt inside ***. For featured patt, skip to Rows 27–29 after ***.

***ROWS 27–28:** B.

ROWS 29–30: A.

ROWS 31–32: B.

ROWS 33–42: A.

ROWS 43–50: D.

ROWS 51–60: A.

ROWS 61–62: B.

ROWS 63–64: A.

ROWS 65–66: B.

ROWS 67–74: A.

ROWS 75–82: B.

ROWS 83–92: A. ***

ROWS 27–90: Rep Rows 11–26 4 times more.

ROWS 91–92: MC.

Cont in St st, work 84 more rows in foll patt:

COLOR PATTERN 3:

ROWS 1–2: CC.

ROWS 3–4: MC.

Rep Rows 1–4 20 times more.

Bind off loosely in last color used.

END SECTIONS (MAKE 2)

Note: These sections will be sewn perpendicular to middle section.

With MC, CO 72 sts.

Working in St st, work in foll patt:

COLOR PATTERN 4:

ROWS 1–10: MC (A).

ROWS 11–18: CC (B).

ROWS 19–26: MC (A).

ROWS 27–58: Rep Rows 11–26 twice more.

ROWS 59–60: MC (A).

Bind off.

FINISHING

Make narrow hems on end sections by rolling Rows 1–2 and Rows 59–60 to underside and loosely stitching in place.

Join side edge of end section to end of middle section.

Rep for other end of scarf. Weave in all ends. Block.

ANOTHER GIFT IDEA
This scarf can be subtly unique or loud and proud if you work the multi-directional sections in different colors.

Embroidered Flower Socks

THESE SWEET GIRLY SOCKS KNIT WITH A SUPERWASH WOOL-AND-NYLON BLEND
YARN ARE GREAT FOR ANY SEASON. Featuring a feminine picot edge around
the cuff and colorful lazy daisy appliqués dancing up the leg, these socks
are bright and festive. They'll look cute with a summery skirt, or peeking
out from under her favorite jeans.

SIZES
S (M, L)

To fit shoe sizes 1–4 (5–7, 8–10)

FINISHED MEASUREMENTS
Foot circumference: 6½ (7½)" (17 [19]cm)

Foot length: 8¼ (9½, 10¼)" (21 [24, 26]cm)

YARN
2 skeins Lorna's Laces Shepherd Sock Yarn
(superwash wool/nylon blend, 57 g, 215 yds [197m])
  color Sage (MC)

1 skein Lorna's Laces Shepherd Sock Yarn in each
of the foll accent colors:
  color Poppy
  color Sunshine

NEEDLES AND NOTIONS
1 set of 5 size US 1 (2.25mm) double-pointed needles

1 set of 5 size US 2 (2.75mm) double-pointed needles

stitch marker

yarn needle

GAUGE
32 sts x 44 rows = 4" (10cm) in St st on size US 2
(2.75mm) needles

TECHNIQUES

K2TOG (KNIT 2 TOGETHER): Dec 1 st by knitting 2 sts tog.

YO (YARN OVER): Wrap the working yarn around the needle clockwise, and knit the next st as usual. This operation creates an eyelet hole in the knitting and inc 1 st.

P2TOG (PURL 2 TOGETHER): Dec 1 st by purling 2 sts tog.

SL ST (SLIP STITCH): Insert the tip of the right needle into the first st on the left needle purlwise and slip the st from the left needle to the right needle without knitting it.

SSK (SLIP, SLIP, KNIT): Dec 1 st by slipping 2 sts knitwise one at a time, inserting the tip of the left needle into both sts and knitting the 2 sts tog.

Socks (make 2)

With MC and size US 1 (2.25mm) needles, CO 48 (60) sts loosely. Join for working in the rnd, dividing sts evenly over 3 DPNs. Place marker at beg of rnd.

SOCK FACING
Work in St st for 1" (3cm).

TURNING RND (PICOT EDGE): Switch to size US 2 (2.75mm) needles, and work edge as foll: * yo, k2tog; rep from * to end of rnd.

Cont in St st until sock measures 1" (3cm) beyond turning round. Fold sock facing to inside.

NEXT RND: Pick up first st of cast-on edge, knit tog with first st on needle. Cont joining cast-on edge to sts on needle to end of rnd to form hem.

Cont in St st until sock measures 6½" (17cm) from picot edge.

DIVIDE FOR HEEL: Remove marker. Place the first 24 (30) sts on 1 needle (heel sts), place rem 24 (30) sts on a holder for instep.

Work 24 (30) heel sts in St st for 16 (24) rows, slipping the first st of each row. End after a purl row.

TURN THE HEEL

ROW 1 (RS): K16 (20), SSK, turn.

ROW 2 (WS): Sl 1, p8 (10), p2tog, turn.

ROW 3 (RS): Sl 1, k8 (10), SSK, turn.

Rep Rows 2–3 until all sts on needle have been worked and 10 (12) sts rem, ending with a WS row.

Remove instep sts from holder and place on a needle.

GUSSET
(RS) Knit across heel sts. With needle 1, pick up 12 sts along selvage edge between heel and instep. With needle 2, knit across 24 (30) instep sts. With needle 3, pick up and knit 12 sts along rem selvage edge, and then knit across 5 (6) sts of heel. You will have 5 (6) sts on your left needle. Pm, then slide these 5 (6) sts onto needle 1. Heel sts are now divided between needles 1 and 3. Needle 1: 17 (18) sts; Needle 2: 24 (30) sts; Needle 3: 17 (18) sts—58 (66) sts total.

DECREASE ROUND

NEEDLE 1: Knit to last 3 sts, k2tog, k1.

NEEDLE 2: Knit.

NEEDLE 3: Knit 1, SSK, knit to end.

Cont in St st, work dec rnd every other rnd until 48 (60) sts rem.

FOOT

Cont in St st until foot measures 6¼ (7½, 8¼)" (16 [19, 21]cm), or 2" (5cm) less than desired length.

BEGIN TOE SHAPING DECREASE ROUND

NEEDLE 1: Knit to last 3 sts, k2tog, k1.

NEEDLE 2: K1, SSK, knit to last 3 sts, k2tog, k1.

NEEDLE 3: K1, SSK, knit to end.

Work dec rnd every other row until 8 sts rem.

FINISHING

Divide rem 8 sts onto 2 needles. Graft tog using Kitchener st.

∞ NOTE ∞

To graft with Kitchener st, line up both sets of live sts on 2 separate needles with the tips facing the same direction. Thread a yarn needle onto the tail of the back piece. Begin by performing the foll steps once: Bring the needle through the first st on the needle closest to you as if to purl, leaving the st on the needle. Then insert the needle through the first st on the back needle as if to knit, leaving the st on the needle. Now you are ready to graft. * Bring the needle through the first st on the front needle as if to knit, slipping the st off the needle. Bring the needle through the next st on the front needle as if to purl, leaving the st on the needle. Then bring the needle through the first st on the back needle as if to purl, sliding the st off the needle. Bring the needle through the next st on the back needle as if to knit, leaving the st on the needle. Rep from * until all sts are grafted tog. Approx every 2" (5cm), tighten up the sts, starting at the beg of the join. Slip the tip of the yarn needle under each leg of each Kitchener st and pull up gently until the tension is correct. Rep across the entire row of grafted sts. It may help you to say to yourself, "Knit, purl – purl, knit" as you go.

EMBROIDERY

Using lazy daisy stitch, create flowers using contrasting colors. Embroider flowers on outside ankle of each sock.

QUICK FIX

If you're reading this, there's a good chance this is—or maybe was is a better tense—your first pair of knitted socks. Maybe you've even finished one of them and find yourself unable to go on. Let yourself off the hook. You can always buy a pair of small-gauge knit socks and embroider them with lazy daisies.

Pinwheel Pillow

I LOVE SHORT ROWS. They made this pillow possible, as round and round it goes in a pinwheel of deep reds with tangerine highlights. Each side of the pillow is worked in one continuous piece. Then the two sides of the pillow are connected with a chunky cable and finished off with covered buttons. It's so much fun to knit out of one of my favorite yarns of all time, The Fibre Company's Khroma. Your sister will carry this around the house as she decides where to put it—this pillow looks great everywhere!

FINISHED MEASUREMENTS
16" (41cm) in diameter, 4" (10cm) "tall"

YARN
2 skeins The Fibre Company Khroma Worsted Weight (alpaca/merino blend, 50 g, 100 yds [91m]) in the foll colors:
   color #04 Pomegranate (A)
   color #05 Winesap (B)
   color #03 Blood Orange (C)

NEEDLES AND NOTIONS
size US 8 (5.0mm) needles

(2) 1½" (4cm) cover buttons

yarn needle

cable needle

waste yarn

16" (41cm) round pillow form

GAUGE
18 sts x 24 rows = 4" (10cm) in St st

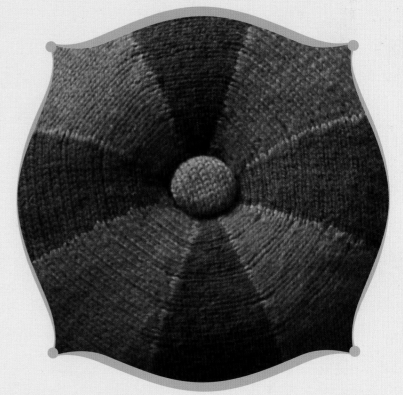

TECHNIQUES

SHORT ROW SHAPING

(RS) WRAP AND TURN (W&T): Wyif, sl 1 st from the left needle to the right. Move yarn to the back, sl st back to the left needle, turn work. 1 st has been wrapped.

(WS) WRAP AND TURN (W&T): Wyib, sl 1 st from the left needle to the right. Move yarn to the front, sl st back to the left needle, turn work. 1 st has been wrapped.

ɷ NOTE ɷ
Whenever you come to a wrap, work the wrap tog with the st it wraps. To pick up a wrap and its st, slide the tip of the right needle into the wrap from the front of the work and place the wrap on the left needle alongside the st it wraps. Knit the 2 loops tog as one st.

C6F (CABLE 6 FRONT): Slip 3 sts to cn and hold to the front of the work. K3, k3 from cn.

C6B (CABLE 6 BACK): Slip 3 sts to cn and hold to the back of the work. K3, k3 from cn.

Pillow

FRONT AND BACK (MAKE 2)
With waste yarn and size US 8 (5.0mm) needles, CO 32 sts.

ɷ NOTE ɷ
To work a provisional cast on, crochet a chain with scrap yarn several chains longer than the number of sts you will be casting on. Cut yarn and tie off crochet chain. Leaving a tail, knit the number of cast-on sts indicated in the patt through the back loops of the crochet chain.

** With yarn A,

ROW 1 (RS): Knit—32 sts.

ROW 2 (WS): P4, w&t.

ROW 3 AND ALL ODD-NUMBERED (RS) ROWS: Knit to end.

ROW 4: P8, w&t.

ROW 6: P12, w&t.

ROW 8: P16, w&t.

ROW 10: P20, w&t.

ROW 12: P24, w&t.

ROW 14: P28, w&t.

ROW 16: P32.

ROW 18: Rep Row 14.

ROW 20: Rep Row 12.

ROW 22: Rep Row 10.

ROW 24: Rep Row 8.

ROW 26: Rep Row 6.

ROW 28: Rep Row 4.

ROW 30: Rep Row 2.

ROW 32: With yarn C, purl to end, working all wraps tog with the wrapped sts—32 sts.

With yarn B, rep Rows 1–31.

With yarn C, Rep Row 32. **

Rep between ** 3 more times, leaving last row (yarn C) on needle. Cut yarn. Remove waste yarn, place sts on a needle. With 18" (46cm) length of yarn A and yarn needle, join sts from both needles using Kitchener st.

ɷ NOTE ɷ
To graft with Kitchener st, line up both sets of live sts on 2 separate needles with the tips facing the same direction. Thread a yarn needle onto the tail of the back piece. Begin by performing the foll steps once: Bring the needle through the first st on the needle closest to you as if to purl, leaving the st on the needle. Then insert the needle through the first st on the back needle as if to knit, leaving the st on the needle. Now you are ready to graft. * Bring the needle through the first st on the front needle as if to knit, slipping the st off the needle. Bring the needle through the next st on the front needle as if to purl, leaving the st on the needle. Then bring the needle through the first st on the back needle as if to purl, sliding the st off the needle. Bring the needle through the next st on the back needle as if to knit, leaving the st on the needle. Rep from * until all sts are grafted tog. Approx every 2" (5cm), tighten up the sts, starting at the beg of the join. Slip the tip of the yarn needle under each leg of each Kitchener st and pull up gently until the tension is correct. Rep across the entire row of grafted sts. It may help you to say to yourself, "Knit, purl – purl, knit" as you go.

SIDE CABLE

With waste yarn, CO 13 sts. With yarn C, work as foll:

ROW 1 (RS): K13.

ROW 2 AND ALL EVEN-NUMBERED (WS) ROWS: P13.

ROW 3: K2, C6F, K5.

ROW 5: K13.

ROW 7: K5, C6B, K2.

ROW 8: P13.

Rep these 8 rows 34 times, or until cable measures 43" (109cm). Remove waste yarn from cast-on end and place sts on a needle. Connect sts on both needles using Kitchener st.

FINISHING

Connect side cable to front and back of pillow using mattress st. See the Glossary, page 141, for instructions on working in mattress st.

When it is three-quarters connected, insert pillow form. Complete mattress st. Weave in ends.

BUTTON COVERS (MAKE 2)

With yarn C and size US 8 (5.0mm) needles, CO 10 sts. Work in St st until piece measures 2" (5cm). BO.

Place knit square over cover button and gather edges tight on the underside of button using yarn needle and yarn C, creating the button cover. Rep for the second button. Place buttons at center of front and back of pillow. With yarn on yarn needle, sew through pillow, catching each button several times and pulling tight so buttons indent on each side. Secure in place.

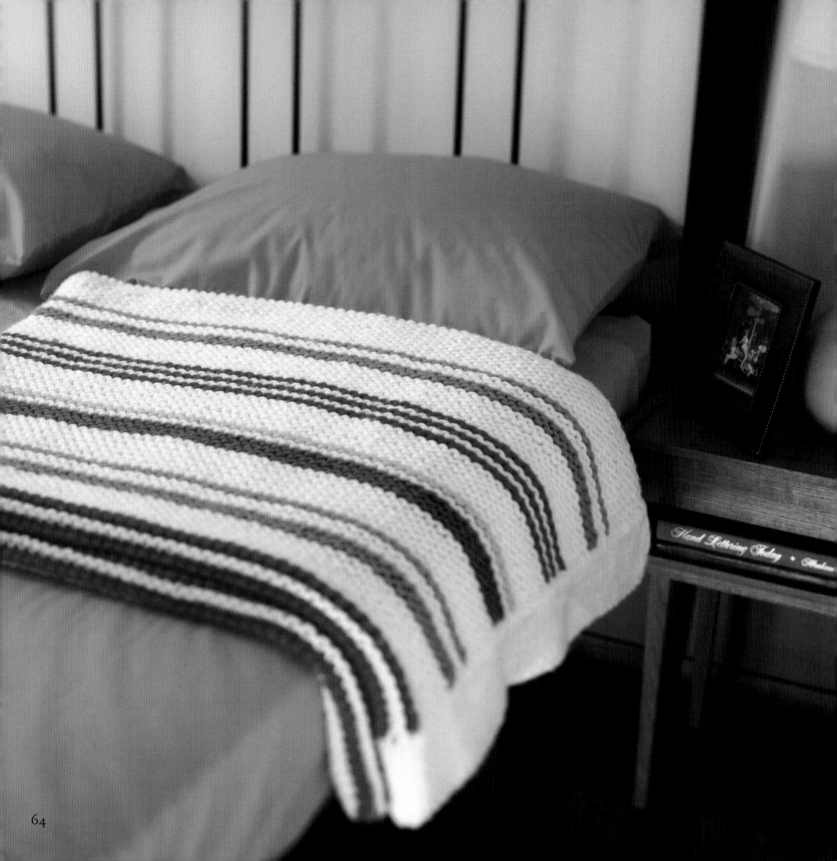

Bright Stripes Throw

IF YOU CAN KNIT IN GARTER STITCH, THEN YOU CAN CREATE THIS SPORTY THROW. Knit on size 15 needles, it is a relatively quick knit for its size with a fun range of colors repeating across. The top edge is finished with a Stockinette stitch border simulating traditional blanket binding. This blanket is a quality piece your sister will treasure throughout her life.

FINISHED MEASUREMENTS
approx 50" x 60" (127cm x 152cm)

YARN
10 skeins Brown Sheep Burly Spun (100% wool, 100 g, 130 yds [119m])
   color # BS10 Cream (MC)

1 skein Brown Sheep Burly Spun in each of the foll colors:
   color #BS78 Aztec Turqoise (CC1)
   color #BS155 Lemon Drop (CC2)
   color #BS180 Ruby Red (CC3)
   color #BS120 Limeade (CC4)
   color #BS110 Orange You Glad (CC5)

NEEDLES AND NOTIONS
24" (60cm) or 40" (102cm) size US 15 (10mm) circular needle

yarn needle

GAUGE
9 sts x 18 rows = 4" (10cm) in garter st

Throw

With size US 15 (10 mm) needles and MC, CO 125 sts. Work in garter st for 17 rows—9 garter ridges.

** **SWITCH TO CC1:** Work in garter st for 6 rows.

SWITCH TO MC: Work in garter st for 2 rows.

SWITCH TO CC2: Work in garter st for 2 rows.

SWITCH TO MC: Work in garter st for 12 rows.

SWITCH TO CC3: Work in garter st for 2 rows.

SWITCH TO MC: Work in garter st for 4 rows.

SWITCH TO CC3: Work in garter st for 2 rows.

SWITCH TO MC: Work in garter st for 12 rows.

SWITCH TO CC4: Work in garter st for 4 rows.

SWITCH TO MC: Work in garter st for 4 rows.

SWITCH TO CC5: Work in garter st for 2 rows.

SWITCH TO MC: Work in garter st for 12 rows.

Rep from ** twice more.

With MC, work 6 rows garter st.

BO loosely.

FINISHING
Weave in all ends from top edge. With RS facing, using size US 15 (10mm) needles and MC, pick up 100 sts evenly spaced along top edge (about 8 sts for every 9 ridges of garter st).

Work in St st for 3½" (9cm), ending with a WS row.

TURNING RIDGE: Purl 1 row on RS.

Work in St st for 3½" (9cm). BO loosely.

Fold edge to back side along turning ridge. Stitch edge into place. Sew the ends of the St st binding closed. Weave in all ends.

Tiered Skirt

THE IDEA OF A KNIT SKIRT CAN DRAW MIXED REACTIONS. I happen to love them. With the right yarn, like this Cascade Pima Tencel, they hang nicely, and they're certainly very comfortable. Your sister can work it all day long in this A-line skirt featuring two tiers accented with ribbon trim.

SIZES
S (M, L)

FINISHED MEASUREMENTS
Skirt waist: 34½ (37, 39½)" (88 [94, 100]cm)

Skirt sits below waist, on hips.

Hem circumference: 44½ (47, 50)" (113 [119, 127]cm)

Length: 24 (24½, 25)" (61 [62, 64]cm)

YARN
10 (12, 14) skeins Cascade Pima Tencel
(Peruvian pima cotton/Tencel blend,
50 g, 109 yds [100m])
  color #2493 Eggplant

NEEDLES AND NOTIONS
24" (61cm) size US 6 (4.0mm) circular needle

24" (61cm) size US 7 (4.5mm) circular needle

waste yarn for provisional cast on

yarn needle

1 yd (1m) of 1½" (4cm) wide elastic

sewing needle

thread

4 yds (4m) 1" (3cm) wide Petersham ribbon

GAUGE
20 sts x 26 rows = 4" (10cm) in St st using larger needles

TECHNIQUES

SSK (SLIP, SLIP, KNIT): Dec 1 st by slipping 2 sts knitwise one at a time, inserting the tip of the left needle into both stst and knitting the 2 sts tog.

K2TOG (KNIT 2 TOGETHER): Dec 1 st by knitting 2 sts tog.

P2TOG (PURL 2 TOGETHER): Dec 1 st by purling 2 sts tog.

Skirt Back and Front (make 2)

BOTTOM LAYER

** With size US 6 (4.0mm) needles and using a provisional cast on, CO 113 (120, 128) sts. Work in St st for 1" (3cm), ending with a WS row. Switch to size US 7 (4.5mm) needles.

∾ NOTE ∾

To work a provisional cast on, crochet a chain with scrap yarn several chains longer than the number of sts you will be casting on. Cut yarn and tie off crochet chain. Leaving a tail, knit the number of cast-on sts indicated in the patt through the back loops of the crochet chain.

TURNING ROW (RS): Purl.

Work in St st for 1" (3cm), ending with a WS row.

TURN HEM

Undo provisional cast on and place live sts on a smaller needle. Fold hem facing under along turning row. **

Join sts from 2 needles as foll: Knit 1st st from top needle and 1st st from bottom needle tog. Cont joining sts from both needles to the end of the row—113 (120, 128) sts.

Work even in St st until piece measures 5" (13cm) from turning row. Place sts on a holder.

TOP LAYER

Rep instructions for bottom layer from ** to **. Place bottom layer sts on a needle and place behind top layer. Join sts from 3 needles as foll: Knit 1st st from all 3 needles tog. Cont joining top layer, cast-on edge and bottom layer tog to the end of the row— 113 (120, 128) sts.

Work even in St st for 3 rows, ending with a WS row.

DEC ROW (RS): K2, SSK, work to last 4 sts, k2tog, k2.

Working in St st, rep this dec row every 12th row 5 (4, 3) times, every 10th row 2 (2, 3) times, every 8th row 2 (3, 3) times, then every 6th row 2 (3, 4) times—89 (94, 100) sts.

Place sts on a holder.

SKIRT FRONT

Make same as skirt back.

WAISTBAND

Place 89 (94, 100) sts from front and 89 (94, 100) sts from back on a size US 7 (4.5mm) circular needle. Join for working in the rnd, placing a marker at the beg of the rnd—178 (188, 200) sts.

JOINING RND (BOTTOM EDGE OF WAISTBAND): Purl, dec 2 sts by p2tog where front and back meet at each side—176 (186, 198) sts.

Work even in St st for 2" (5cm), ending with a WS rnd.

TURNING RND: Purl.

Switch to size US 6 (4.0mm) needles. Work in St st for 2" (5cm).

BO loosely.

FINISHING

Join side seams of skirt front and back using mattress st. See the Glossary, page 141, for instructions on working in mattress st.

Turn waistband facing under at turning rnd. Stitch in place until 6" (15cm) rem open. Insert elastic through formed casing. Fit, cut and stitch ends of elastic. Finish stitching the waistband in place.

Weave in all ends.

Measure circumference of hems on bottom layer and top layer. Cut 2 ribbons to the measured lengths plus 1" (3cm). Sew seams in ribbons to form circles, leaving ½" (1cm) seam allowances. Wet ribbon and iron flat, ironing seams open. With sewing thread, whipstitch each circle of ribbon to the WS of bottom edge of each hem, creating ½" (1cm) reveal of ribbon below knit hems.

TIERED SKIRT
WOMEN'S S (M, L)

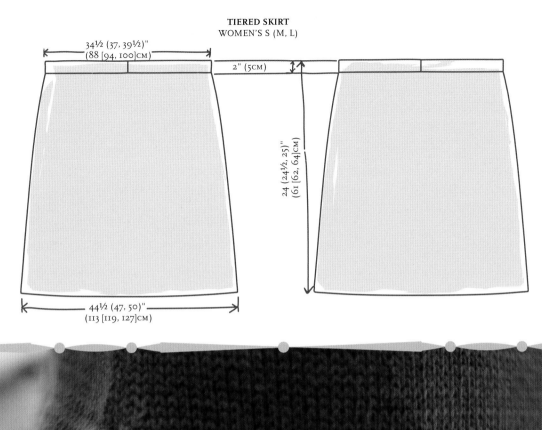

34½ (37, 39½)"
(88 [94, 100]CM)

2" (5CM)

24 (24½, 25)"
(61 [62, 64]CM)

44½ (47, 50)"
(113 [119, 127]CM)

Men in Our Lives

My husband and I recently bought our first house. As I was shuffling all our stuff around, I came across one of the first sweaters I ever knit for Abe. The pattern was from a popular knitting magazine, and the sweater features beautiful cables, seed stitch everywhere, the works. I was so proud of myself after I completed that. It has mohair in it, and I remember the moment when Abe slipped it over his head. I could totally tell he was thinking, okay, my wife just spent months making this for me but this sweater weighs 500 pounds and I'm already itching like crazy—I never want to wear it. Also, the neck was very tight, so I cut it off. When I took it out of the box after moving into our house, it was still missing the neck.

What I have come to realize since then is this: When it comes to knitwear, men like the basics. Every project in this chapter has met with Abe's approval, so you can proceed with confidence. Try out the *Simple Sweater* (see page 84) or the *Rustic Sweater Vest* (see page 88) for easy sweater gift giving. Maybe he would like a pair of *Man Socks* (see page 80) or a ribbed scarf (see page 78). Is he a city man? He might like the *Urban Beanie* with a subtle earflap to keep his lobes warm (see page 74). Abe is a juggler (clarification: not his profession; he just happens to know how to juggle), and if your man also juggles, look no further than the knit *Juggling Balls* (see page 72) in bright autumn colors. No matter how particular your guy is, there is something here he can appreciate.

Juggling Balls

ABE AND I CAME TO A REALIZATION RECENTLY. IT WOULD SEEM THERE IS
A CONNECTION BETWEEN GIRLS WHO KNIT AND BOYS WHO JUGGLE. If your
man doesn't juggle yet, why not set him up with these juggling balls and
an instructional guide? Think of the entertainment!

YARN
1 skein Rowan Scottish Tweed 4-ply (100% wool, 25 g,
120 yds [110m]) in each of the foll colors:
  color #018 Thatch (A)
  color #011 Sunset (B)
  color #015 Apple (C)

NEEDLES AND NOTIONS
size US 3 (3.25mm) needles

yarn needle

dry beans

GAUGE
26 sts x 38 rows = 4" (10cm) in St st

		C	C			
		C	C			2" (5cm)
B	B	A	A	B	B	
B	B	A	A	B	B	4" (10cm)
		C	C			
		C	C			6" (15cm)
		A	A			
		A	A			8" (20cm)

Juggling Balls (make 3)
With yarn B, CO 15 sts.

Work in St st until piece measures 2" (5cm) from cast-on edge.

SWITCH TO YARN C: Knit in St st until piece measures 4" (10cm).

SWITCH TO YARN B: Knit in St st until piece measures 6" (15cm).

SWITCH TO YARN C: Knit in St st until piece measures 8" (20cm).

Fasten off. Leave a long yarn tail for sewing.

With yarn A, pick up 15 sts along one side of the top color B
block (2" [5cm] from top). Knit in St st for 2" (5cm). Fasten
off, leaving a long tail.

Rep on other side of same color B block.

FINISHING
Sew up cubes on all sides but one with mattress st. See the
Glossary, page 141, for instructions on working in mattress st.

Fill with dry beans. Sew up final side. Weave in ends.

Urban Beanie

THIS URBAN-STYLE HAT FITS SNUG TO THE HEAD AND HAS JUST ENOUGH EARFLAP TO GET THE JOB DONE. Your man will be the warmest trendsetter in town! Pair this hat with the *One-by-One Ribbed Scarf* (see page 78) to make a nice gifty set.

FINISHED MEASUREMENTS
8¼" (21cm) high x 14" (36cm) around (unstretched)

YARN
2 skeins The Fibre Company Organik (organic NZ wool/baby alpaca/silk blend, 50 g, 85 yds [78m])
　　color #190 Chocolate Brown

ANOTHER GIFT IDEA: VARIATION HAT
1 skein Cascade 220 (100% Peruvian Highland wool, 220 yds [200m])
　　color #4002 gray

NEEDLES AND NOTIONS
16" (41cm) size US 6 (4.0mm) circular needle

size US 6 (4.0mm) double-pointed needles

yarn needle

marker

GAUGE
29 sts x 28 rows = 4" (10cm) in k1, p1 ribbing (unstretched)

TECHNIQUES

M1 (MAKE 1): Inc 1 st by picking up, from front to back, the bar between the next st and the st just knit and placing it on the left needle. Knit into the back of the picked-up st. (In this patt, this is identified as m1 knitwise.)

M1 (MAKE 1 PURLWISE): Inc 1 st by picking up, from back to front, the bar between the next st and the st just knit and placing it on the left needle. Knit into the front of the picked-up st.

SL ST (SLIP STITCH): Insert the tip of the right needle into the first st on the left needle purlwise and slip the st from the left needle to the right needle without knitting it.

K2TOG (KNIT 2 TOGETHER): Dec 1 st by knitting 2 sts tog.

Hat

EARFLAPS (MAKE 2)
With size US 6 (4.0mm) needles and MC, CO 7 sts.

ROW 1 (RS): Wyif, sl 1 purlwise (on this and each foll row of earflap), * p1, k1; rep from * to end of row—7 sts.

ROW 2 (WS): Sl 1, * k1, p1, rep from * to end of row.

ROW 3: Sl 1, m1 knitwise, rib to last st, m1 knitwise, k1—9 sts.

ROW 4: Sl 1, p1, rib to last 2 sts, p2.

ROW 5: Sl 1, m1 purlwise, rib to last st, m1 purlwise, k1—11 sts.

ROW 6: Sl 1, rib to end of row.

Break off yarn. Place sts on a holder.

HAT
Using size US 6 (4.0 mm) circular needle, CO 20 sts, rib across 11 earflap sts, CO 39, rib across 11 earflap sts, CO 19—100 sts.

Pm, join for working in the rnd. Work in k1, p1 ribbing until piece measures 8" (20cm), or desired length before top shaping.

TOP OF HAT

cʒ NOTE cʒ
Change to size US 6 (4.0mm) DPNs when necessary.

RND 1: * K2tog, rep from * to end of rnd—50 sts.

RND 2: Knit.

RND 3: Rep Rnd 1—25 sts.

RND 4: Knit.

RND 5: * K2tog, rep from * to last st, k1—13 sts.

Break yarn. Thread through yarn needle and pull tight through rem sts. Weave in ends.

ANOTHER GIFT IDEA
The beanie at right is knit in a smoky charcoal yarn. Add simple leather ties or knit I-cord ties for a different look.

One-by-One Ribbed Scarf

THIS SCARF HAS PROVED TRIED AND TRUE ON ACTUAL MEN! Made with Noro Silk Garden yarn in a graduated brown-and-black colorway, it is very warm, comfortable and manly. It looks great with a dressy overcoat, a casual hoodie, or even just a T-shirt!

FINISHED MEASUREMENTS
approx 5½" x 64" (14cm x 163cm)

YARN
3 skeins Noro Silk Garden (silk/kid mohair/lambswool blend, 50 g, 109 yds [100m])
color #47 brown-and-black colorway

NEEDLES AND NOTIONS
size US 9 (5.5mm) straight or circular needles

yarn needle

GAUGE
27 sts x 21 rows = 4" x 4" (10cm x 10cm) in k1, p1 ribbing (unstretched)

Scarf

With size US 9 (5.5mm) needles and Noro Silk Garden, CO 38 sts.

ಀ NOTE ಀ
For neater selvages, always slip first st as if to purl, with yarn in back.

ROW 1: Sl 1, * p1, k1, rep from * to last st, p1.

Rep Row 1 for rib pattern until scarf measures 64" (163cm) or desired length.

BO in rib. Weave in ends.

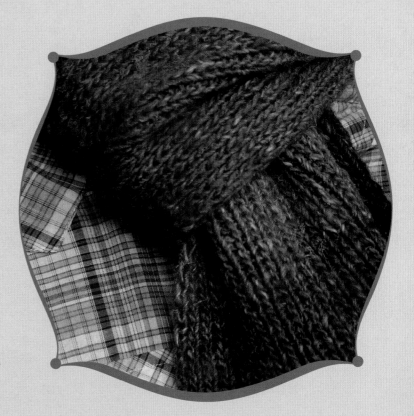

TECHNIQUES
SL (SLIP STITCH): Pass 1 st purlwise from left needle to right needle without knitting it.

Man Socks

THE FIRST THING I EVER KNIT FOR MY HUSBAND WAS A PAIR OF SOCKS. At the time, I didn't understand the importance of gauge, and I knit the fingering weight yarn pattern with heavy worsted weight yarn. Needless to say, the resulting socks were freakish, so big they looked like they were meant to be worn on the outside of his work boots. So, if you would like to attempt some socks for your man, take my advice: Check your gauge. I intentionally designed this pattern for worsted weight yarn, so you can use a nice manly yarn and still have your socks come out the right size. Enjoy!

SIZES
S (M, L)

FINISHED MEASUREMENTS
Foot circumference: approx 8½" (21cm)

The foot circumference given fits most men.

Foot length: 9½ (10¼, 11)" (24 [26, 28]cm)

YARN
2 skeins Peace Fleece Yarn (mohair/wool blend, 114 g, 200 yds [183m])
    color Father's Grey

NEEDLES AND NOTIONS
size US 6 (4.0mm) double-pointed needles

yarn needle

GAUGE
18 sts x 28 rows = 4" (10cm) in St st

TECHNIQUES
SSK (SLIP, SLIP, KNIT): Dec 1 st by slipping 2 sts knitwise one at a time from the left needle to the right needle. Insert the tip of the left needle into the front of both sts and knit the 2 sts tog.

P2TOG (PURL 2 TOGETHER): Dec 1 st by purling 2 sts tog.

SL ST (SLIP STITCH): Insert the tip of the right needle into the first st on the left needle purlwise and slip the st from the left needle to the right needle without knitting it.

K2TOG (KNIT 2 TOGETHER): Dec 1 st by knitting 2 sts tog.

Socks (make 2)

With size US 6 (4.0mm) DPNs, CO 40 sts loosely. Divide sts over 3 needles. Join for working in the rnd, taking care not to twist sts. Work in k1, p1 rib for 9" (23cm).

Sl first 20 sts onto 1 needle. These will be the heel sts. Place rem 20 sts on a holder. These will be the instep sts.

Work 20 heel sts in St st for 16 rows, sl the first st at the beg of each row. End after a WS row.

TURN HEEL

SET-UP ROW (RS): K13, SSK, turn.

ROW 1: P7, p2tog.

ROW 2: K7, SSK, turn.

Rep Rows 1–2 until all sts are worked across row—8 sts rem. You will finish after a WS row.

WORK GUSSET
Knit across 8 heel sts.

NEEDLE 1: Pick up 12 sts between heel and instep sts.

NEEDLE 2: Knit across 20 instep sts.

NEEDLE 3: Pick up 12 sts between instep and heel. Knit 4 sts of heel. Pm and sl rem 4 sts of heel onto needle 1—52 sts total.

DEC RND

NEEDLE 1: Knit to last 3 sts, k2tog, k1.

NEEDLE 2: Knit to end of needle.

NEEDLE 3: K1, SSK, knit to end of needle.

Rep this dec rnd every other rnd until 36 sts rem.

Work straight in St st for 2" (5cm).

INC RND

NEEDLE 1: Knit to last 2 sts, m1, k2.

NEEDLE 2: K2, m1, knit to last 2 sts, m1, k2.

NEEDLE 3: K2, m1, knit to end of needle—40 sts.

Work straight in St st for 7½ (8¼, 9)" (19 [21, 23]cm), or until foot measures 2" (5cm) less than desired length.

TOE

DEC RND

NEEDLE 1: Knit to last 3 sts, k2tog, k1.

NEEDLE 2: K1, SSK, knit to last 3 sts, k2tog, k1.

NEEDLE 3: K1, SSK, knit to end of needle.

Work this dec rnd every other rnd until 20 sts rem.

NEEDLE 1: Knit to last 3 sts, k2tog, k1.

NEEDLE 2: SSK, k2tog.

NEEDLE 3: K1, SSK, knit to end of needle—16 sts rem.

Divide sts evenly on 2 needles.

Graft sts from 2 needles tog using Kitchener st.

✑ NOTE ✑

To graft with Kitchener st, line up both sets of live sts on 2 needles with the tips facing the same direction. Thread a yarn needle onto the tail of the back piece. Begin by performing the foll steps once: Bring the needle through the first st on the needle closest to you as if to purl, leaving the st on the needle. Then insert the needle through the first st on the back needle as if to knit, leaving the st on the needle. Now you are ready to graft. * Bring the needle through the first st on the front needle as if to knit, slipping the st off the needle. Bring the needle through the next st on the front needle as if to purl, leaving the st on the needle. Then bring the needle through the first st on the back needle as if to purl, sliding the st off the needle. Bring the needle through the next st on the back needle as if to knit, leaving the st on the needle. Rep from * until all sts are grafted tog. Approx every 2" (5cm), tighten up the sts, starting at the beg of the join. Slip the tip of the yarn needle under each leg of each Kitchener st and pull up gently until the tension is correct. Rep across the entire row of grafted sts. It may help you to say to yourself, "Knit, purl – purl, knit" as you go.

Weave in all ends.

Simple Sweater

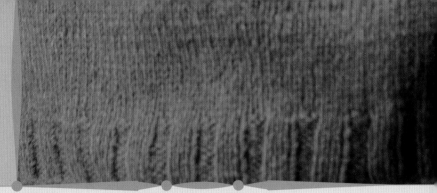

IF YOU HAVE NEVER KNIT WITH PEACE FLEECE, YOU ARE GOING TO LOVE IT, STARTING WITH THE FABULOUS ARRAY OF COLORS TO CHOOSE FROM. You'll enjoy knitting this basic pullover up from the hem, and when you finish, you'll get to enjoy the best part—watching this cozy sweater work itself into your guy's regular outfit rotation. This wool-blend yarn is a perfect weight to wear around the house, for going out, or on a crisp fall day.

SIZES
S (M, L, XL)

To fit chest sizes 36 (40, 44, 48)" (91 [102, 112, 122]cm)

FINISHED MEASUREMENTS
Chest circumference: 42 (46, 50, 54)" (107 [117, 127, 137]cm)

Length: 26½ (26½, 27, 27)" (67 [67, 69, 69]cm)

Armhole depth: 10 (10⅛, 10¾, 11)" (25 [26, 27, 28]cm)

YARN
7 (8, 8, 9) skeins Peace Fleece Worsted Weight
(mohair/wool blend, 114 g, approx 200 yds [183m])
color Shaba

TECHNIQUES
SSK (SLIP, SLIP, KNIT): Dec 1 st by slipping 2 sts knitwise one at a time from the left needle to the right needle. Insert the tip of the left needle into the front of both sts and knit the 2 sts tog.

K2TOG (KNIT 2 TOGETHER): Dec 1 st by knitting 2 sts tog.

M1 (MAKE 1): Inc 1 st by picking up, from front to back, the bar between the next st and the st just knit and placing it on the left needle. Knit into the back of the picked-up st.

NEEDLES AND NOTIONS
16" (41cm) size US 7 (4.5mm) circular needle

24" (61cm) size US 7 (4.5mm) circular needle

24" (61cm) size US 8 (5.0mm) circular needle

yarn needle

GAUGE
16 sts x 26 rows = 4" (10cm) in St st using larger size needle

Sweater

BACK
With size US 7 (4.5mm) 24" (61cm) circular needle, cast on 82 (92, 102, 107) sts.

ROW 1: K1, * k3, p2; rep from * to last st, k1.

ROW 2: P1, * k2, p3; rep from * to last st, p1.

Rep Rows 1–2 until piece measures 2" (5cm) from cast-on edge—12 rows total.

Switch to size US 8 (5.0mm) 24" (61cm) circular needle. Work in St st, inc 4 (2, 0, 3) sts evenly spaced on first knit row—86 (94, 102, 110) sts.

Work even in St st until piece measures 15 (15, 15, 15¾)" (38 [38, 38, 40]cm) from cast-on edge, or until desired length.

BEGIN ARMHOLE SHAPING

Bind off 3 (4, 5, 5) sts at beg of next 2 rows—80 (86, 92, 100) sts.

DEC ROW: K2, SSK, knit to last 4 sts, k2tog, k2—78 (84, 90, 98) sts.

Rep dec row EOR 2 (3, 4, 4) times more—74 (78, 82, 90) sts.

Rep dec row EOR every 4th row twice—70 (74, 78, 86) sts.

Rep dec row every 8th row 2 (2, 1, 3) times—66 (70, 76, 80) sts.

Work even in St st until piece measures 24 (24, 25⅜, 25⅜)" (61 [61, 65, 65]cm) from beg, ending after a WS row.

BEGIN NECK SHAPING

K24 (26, 28, 30), BO 18 (18, 20, 20) sts, k24 (26, 28, 30). Working each side separately, cont to work on left side as foll:

ROW 1 (WS): Purl—24 (26, 28, 30) sts.

ROW 2 (RS): BO 4 (5, 6, 6) sts, knit to end—20 (21, 22, 24) sts.

ROW 3: Purl.

ROW 4: BO 1, knit to end—19 (20, 21, 23) sts.

BEGIN SHOULDER SHAPING

ROW 5 (WS): BO 6 (6, 6, 7) sts, purl to end—13 (14, 15, 16) sts.

ROW 6: BO 1, knit to end—12 (13, 14, 15) sts.

ROW 7: BO 6 (6, 5, 7) sts, purl to end—6 (7, 9, 8) sts.

ROW 8: BO 1, knit to end—5 (6, 8, 7) sts.

BO rem 5 (6, 8, 7) sts.

Reattach ball at neck edge to right side.

ROW 1 (WS): Purl—24 (26, 28, 30) sts.

ROW 2 (RS): Knit to end.

ROW 3 (WS): BO 4 (5, 6, 6) sts, purl to end—20 (21, 22, 24) sts.

ROW 4: Knit.

ROW 5: BO 1, purl to end—19 (20, 21, 23) sts.

BEGIN SHOULDER SHAPING

ROW 6 (RS): BO 6 (6, 6, 7) sts, knit to end—13 (14, 15, 16) sts.

ROW 7: BO 1, purl to end—12 (13, 14, 15) sts.

ROW 8: BO 6 (6, 5, 7) sts, knit to end—6 (7, 9, 8) sts.

ROW 9: BO 1, purl to end—5 (6, 8, 7) sts.

BO rem 5 (6, 8, 7) sts.

FRONT

Work same as for back until piece measures 22½ (22½, 23⅜, 23⅜)" (57 [57, 59, 59] cm) from cast-on edge, ending with a WS row.

BEGIN NECK SHAPING

K26 (28, 30, 32), BO 14 (14, 16, 16) sts, k26 (28, 30, 32) sts. Working each side separately, cont working on left side as foll:

NEXT ROW: P1 row—26 (28, 30, 32) sts.

NEXT ROW (RS): BO 2, knit to end—24 (26, 28, 30) sts.

Rep this dec on RS at neck edge twice more—20 (22, 24, 26) sts.

NEXT ROW: Purl.

NEXT ROW: BO 1, knit to end—19 (21, 23, 25) sts.

Rep this dec on RS at neck edge 2 (3, 4, 4) times more—17 (18, 19, 21) sts.

SIZE SMALL ONLY: Work 2 rows even in St st.

BEGIN SHOULDER SHAPING

ROW 1 (WS): BO 6 (6, 6, 7) sts, purl to end—11 (12, 13, 14) sts.

ROW 2: Knit.

ROW 3: BO 6 (6, 5, 7) sts, purl to end—5 (6, 8, 7) sts.

ROW 4: Knit to end.

BO rem 5 (6, 8, 7) sts.

Reattach yarn at neck edge to right side.

Purl 1 row, knit 1 row—26 (28, 30, 32) sts.

DEC ROW: BO 2, purl to end—24 (26, 28, 30) sts.

Rep dec row at neck edge on WS twice more—20 (22, 24, 26) sts.

Knit 1 row.

DEC ROW: BO 1, purl to end—19 (21, 23, 25) sts.

Rep this dec row at neck edge 2 (3, 4, 4) times more—17 (18, 19, 21) sts.

SIZE SMALL ONLY: Work 2 rows even in St st.

BEGIN SHOULDER SHAPING

ROW 1 (RS): BO 6 (6, 6, 7) sts, knit to end—11 (12, 13, 14) sts.

ROW 2: Purl.

ROW 3: BO 6 (6, 5, 7) sts, knit to end—5 (6, 8, 7) sts.

ROW 4: Purl.

BO rem 5 (6, 8, 7) sts.

SLEEVES (MAKE 2)

With size US 7 (4.5mm) 24" (61cm) circular needle, CO 42 (42, 47, 47) sts.

ROW 1: K1, * k3, p2; rep from * to last st, k1.

ROW 2: P1, * k2, p3; rep from * to last st, p1.

Rep Rows 1–2 until piece measures 2" (5cm) from cast-on edge—12 rows total.

Switch to size US 8 (5.0mm) 24" (61cm) circular needle.

INC ROW: K2, m1, knit to last 2 sts, m1, k2—44 (44, 49, 49) sts.

Cont in St st, working inc row every 6th row 11 (13, 12, 15) times more—66 (70, 73, 79) sts.

Work even in St st until sleeve measures 17⅞ (18⅜, 18⅛, 17⅞)" (45 [47, 46, 45]cm), from cast-on edge.

BEGIN CAP SHAPING

BO 3 (4, 5, 5) sts at beg of next 2 rows—60 (62, 63, 69) sts.

DEC ROW: K2, SSK, knit to last 4 sts, k2tog, k2—58 (60, 61, 67) sts.

Rep dec row every RS row 14 (15, 15, 16) times more—30 (30, 31, 35) sts.

Work dec row every 4th row 3 (3, 3, 3) times—24 (24, 25, 29) sts.

BO 0 (0, 0, 2) sts at beg of next 2 rows—24 (24, 25, 25) sts.

BO 3 sts at beg of next 4 rows—12 (12, 13, 13) sts.

BO rem 12 (12, 13, 13) sts.

FINISHING

Join front to back at shoulders. Join sleeve cap to body. Join underarm and side seams with mattress st. See the Glossary, page 141, for instructions on working in mattress st.

Pick up and knit an even number of sts evenly spaced around the neck edge with size US 7 (4.5mm) 16" (41cm) circular needle. Work in k1, p1 ribbing for 1" (3cm). BO loosely.

Weave in all ends.

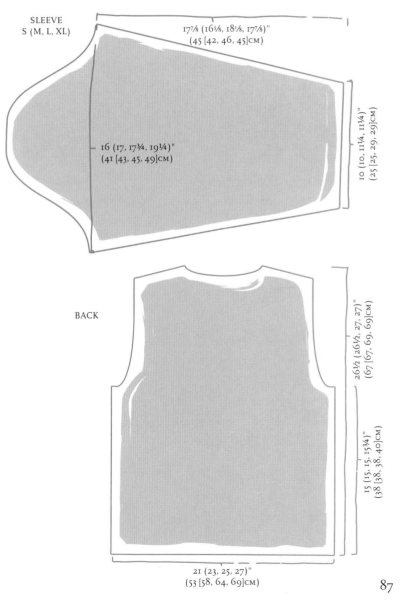

SLEEVE
S (M, L, XL)

17⅞ (16⅝, 18⅛, 17⅞)"
(45 [42, 46, 45]CM)

16 (17, 17¾, 19¼)"
(41 [43, 45, 49]CM)

10 (10, 11¼, 11¼)"
(25 [25, 29, 29]CM)

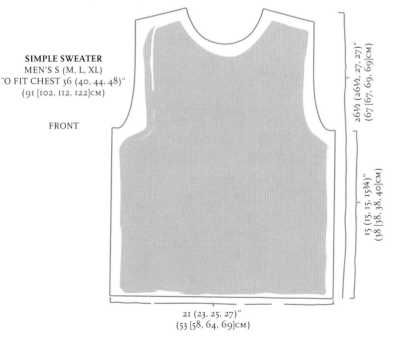

SIMPLE SWEATER
MEN'S S (M, L, XL)
TO FIT CHEST 36 (40, 44, 48)"
(91 [102, 112, 122]CM)

FRONT

26½ (26½, 27, 27)"
(67 [67, 69, 69]CM)

15 (15, 15, 15¾)"
(38 [38, 38, 40]CM)

21 (23, 25, 27)"
(53 [58, 64, 69]CM)

BACK

26½ (26½, 27, 27)"
(67 [67, 69, 69]CM)

15 (15, 15, 15¾)"
(38 [38, 38, 40]CM)

21 (23, 25, 27)"
(53 [58, 64, 69]CM)

Rustic Sweater Vest

ARE YOU FEELING INTIMIDATED ABOUT KNITTING AN ENTIRE SWEATER WITH
SLEEVES AND EVERYTHING? Or maybe your man overheats in sweaters. Try
this vest! The blend of wool, alpaca and viscose in a dk weight yarn keeps the
finished vest nice and light. The tweedy color adds interest to this basic V-neck
pullover. Worn with jeans and a T-shirt or dressed up with a collared shirt, he
will be looking and feeling fine—fall, winter and spring!

SIZES
S (M, L, XL)

To fit chest sizes 36 (40, 44, 48)" (91 [102, 112, 122]cm)

FINISHED MEASUREMENTS
Chest circumference: 42 (46, 50, 54)" (107 [117, 127, 137]cm)

Length: 25 (25½, 25⅞, 26⅛)" (64 [65, 66, 66]cm)

Armhole depth (with bands): 8⅞ (9⅜, 9¾, 10⅛)"
(23 [24, 25, 26]cm)

YARN
6 (6, 6, 7) skeins Rowan Felted Tweed
(merino/alpaca/viscose blend, 50 g, 191 yds [175m])
    color #154 Ginger

NEEDLES AND NOTIONS
16" (41cm) size US 4 (3.5mm) circular needle

24" (61cm) size US 4 (3.5mm) circular needle

24" (61cm) size US 5 (3.75mm) circular needle

markers

yarn needle

GAUGE
24 sts x 32 rows = 4" (10cm) in St st with larger size needle

TECHNIQUES

SSK (SLIP, SLIP, KNIT): Dec 1 st by slipping 2 sts knitwise one at a time from the left needle to the right needle. Insert the tip of the left needle into the front of both sts and knit the 2 sts tog.

K2TOG (KNIT 2 TOGETHER): Dec 1 st by knitting 2 sts tog.

P2TOG (PURL 2 TOGETHER): Dec 1 st by purling 2 sts tog.

P2SSO (PASS 2 SLIPPED STITCHES OVER): Slip 2 sts tog knitwise from the left needle to the right needle. K1, then pass the 2 slipped sts over the knit st.

Vest

BACK

With size US 4 (3.5mm) 24" (61cm) circular needle, CO 128 (140, 152, 164) sts. Work in k1, p1 ribbing for 3" (8cm), ending with a WS row.

Switch to size US 5 (3.75mm) 24" (61cm) circular needle. Work in St st until back measures 14¼ (14⅛, 14, 13⅝)" (36 [36, 36, 35]cm) from cast-on edge, ending with a WS row.

ARMHOLE SHAPING

BO 6 (8, 8, 8) sts at beg of next 2 rows—116 (124, 136, 148) sts.

BO 2 (4, 4, 4) sts at beg of next 2 (2, 4, 6) rows—112 (116, 120, 124) sts.

DEC ROW: K2, SSK, knit to last 4 sts, k2tog, k2—110 (114, 118, 122) sts.

Rep dec row EOR 7 times more—96 (100, 104, 108) sts.

Rep dec row every 4th row 3 times—90 (94, 98, 102) sts.

Rep dec row every 6th row once—88 (92, 96, 100) sts.

Rep dec row every 10th row once—86 (90, 94, 98) sts.

Work even in St st until armhole measures 9⅜ (10, 10½, 11⅛)" (24 [25, 27, 28]cm).

BEGIN NECK AND SHOULDER SHAPING

K32 (33, 35, 36), BO 22 (24, 24, 26) sts, k32 (33, 35, 36). Place right shoulder sts on holder.

Work left shoulder as foll:

ROW 1: Purl across back to neck edge.

ROW 2 (RS): BO 5 sts at neck edge, knit to end—27 (28, 30, 31) sts.

ROW 3: Purl across back to neck edge.

ROW 4: BO 4 sts at neck edge, knit to end—23 (24, 26, 27) sts.

ROW 5: Purl across back to neck edge.

ROW 6: K1, k2tog, knit to end—22 (23, 25, 26) sts.

ROW 7 (WS): BO 7 (7, 8, 8) sts, purl to end—15 (16, 17, 18) sts.

ROW 8: K1, k2tog, knit to end—14 (15, 16, 17) sts.

ROW 9 (WS): BO 7 (7, 8, 8) sts, purl to end—7 (8, 8, 9) sts.

ROW 10: K1, k2tog, knit to end—6 (7, 7, 8) sts.

NEXT ROW (WS): BO rem 6 (7, 7, 8) sts.

RIGHT SHOULDER

Reattach yarn at neck edge.

ROW 1 (WS): BO 5 sts at neck edge, purl to end—27 (28, 30, 31) sts.

ROW 2: Knit across.

ROW 3: BO 4 sts at neck edge, purl to end—23 (24, 26, 27) sts.

ROW 4: Knit across.

ROW 5: P1, p2tog, purl to end—22 (23, 25, 26) sts.

ROW 6 (RS): BO 7 (7, 8, 8,) sts, knit to end—15 (16, 17, 18) sts.

ROW 7: P1, p2tog, purl to end—14 (15, 16, 17) sts.

ROW 8: BO 7 (7, 8, 8) sts, knit to end—7 (8, 8, 9) sts.

ROW 9: P1, p2tog, purl to end—6 (7, 7, 8) sts.

NEXT ROW (RS): BO rem 6 (7, 7, 8) sts.

FRONT

Work as for back until armhole dec are completed to point of "EOR 7 times more"—96 (100, 104, 108) sts. Then rep dec row every 4th row twice—92 (96, 100, 104) sts.

Work 3 rows even, ending with a WS row.

BEGIN NECK SHAPING

∾ NOTE ∾
As you begin neck shaping, cont with armhole shaping.

Pm at center front—46 (48, 50, 52) sts on each side of marker.

AT THE SAME TIME, work neck decrease as foll:

(RS) RIGHT SHOULDER: K2, SSK, knit to 3 sts before neck edge (marker), SSK, k1.

LEFT SHOULDER: Attaching separate ball of yarn, K1, k2tog, knit to 4 sts before end, k2tog, k2.

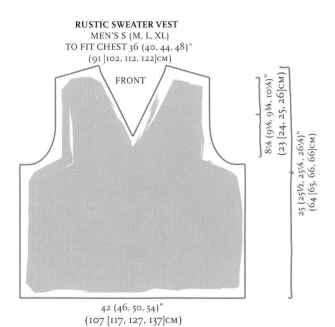

RUSTIC SWEATER VEST
MEN'S S (M, L, XL)
TO FIT CHEST 36 (40, 44, 48)"
(91 [102, 112, 122]CM)

FRONT

8⅞ (9⅜, 9¾, 10⅛)"
(23 [24, 25, 26]CM)

25 (25½, 25⅞, 26⅛)"
(64 [65, 66, 66]CM)

42 (46, 50, 54)"
(107 [117, 127, 137]CM)

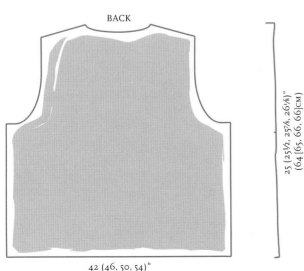

BACK

25 (25½, 25⅞, 26⅛)"
(64 [65, 66, 66]CM)

42 (46, 50, 54)"
(107 [117, 127, 137]CM)

Rep this dec at each side of neck edge EOR 16 times more, then every 3rd row 6 (7, 7, 8) times—20 (21, 23, 24) sts.

Cont to work each side at the same time, using separate balls of yarn, AND CONT ARMHOLE DEC every 6th row once, then every 10th row once, while dec for the neck edge.

Work even in St st, if necessary, until front is same length as back to first bound-off row at armhole edge.

SHOULDER SHAPING

∾ NOTE ∾
Unless otherwise indicated, if working on RS, knit sts for left shoulder; on WS, purl sts for right shoulder.

ROW 1 (RS) R SHOULDER: BO 7 (7, 8, 8) sts, knit to end—13 (14, 15, 16) sts.

ROW 2 (WS) L SHOULDER: BO 7 (7, 8, 8) sts, purl to end—13 (14, 15, 16) sts.

ROW 3 R SHOULDER: BO 7 (7, 8, 8) sts, knit to end—6 (7, 7, 8) sts.

ROW 4 L SHOULDER: BO 7 (7, 8, 8) sts, purl to end—6 (7, 7, 8) sts.

ROW 5 R SHOULDER: BO 6 (7, 7, 8) sts; L shoulder: BO 6 (7, 7, 8) sts.

FINISHING
Join front to back at shoulders. Join side seams using mattress st. See the Glossary, page 141, for instructions on working in mattress st.

ARMHOLE BANDS
With size US 4 (3.5mm) 16" (41cm) circular needle, pick up and knit an even number of sts, evenly spaced, around each armhole. Work in k1, p1 ribbing for 1" (3cm). BO loosely.

NECK BAND
With size US 4 (3.5mm) 16" (41cm) circular needle, starting at a shoulder seam, pick up and knit an even number of sts around neck, including a m1 at center of V which will be kept as a knit st. (Mark this center st.) Pm at beg of rnd. Work in k1, p1 ribbing 1 rnd.

DEC RND: Work in k1, p1 ribbing until 1 st before center marked st, sl2tog knitwise, work 1, p2sso. Cont in ribbing to end of rnd.

Work 1 rnd even in ribbing.

Rep dec rnd every other rnd twice more. BO loosely.

Weave in all ends.

Wee Ones

MY MEMORY OF BEING A WEE ONE IS WRAPPED
UP IN THE KNITWEAR MY GRANDMOTHER CRANKED
OUT FOR ME AND ALL OF MY COUSINS. I particularly
remember a pink cardigan with white cats on the front,
which is where I took inspiration for the cardigan in this
chapter (see page 108). Nostalgia for my late '70s–early
'80s childhood also shows itself in the *Patchwork Blanket*
(see page 114), and in the mitts connected by an I-cord for
running through your jacket (see page 94). Remember
wet mittens hanging from your coat sleeves after playing
in the snow all day?

I have also watched my friend Colleen collect vintage
clothes for her daughter, Honey, and the cuteness is
always in the details. I tried to bring that precious detail
to the wee *Heart-Patch Pants* (see page 104). There is also
a simple vest featuring a kangaroo graphic (see page 98),
perfect for the hippest kids in town.

Creating handmade gifts for wee ones is a classic
thing to do. Enjoy taking part in this timeless ritual.

Square-Top Hat and Mitts

I BOUGHT A SQUARE VELOUR HAT FOR MY NIECE IN SAN FRANCISCO SHORTLY AFTER SHE WAS BORN, AND IT WAS THE CUTEST THING EVER. When you put it on her little head, the corners stuck out like ears. This Dale of Norway version is my answer to that hat. Trust me, it's a total crowd pleaser! Add a pair of precious mitts (no thumbs!) connected with an I-cord that can be threaded through the wee one's jacket to complete this sweet set.

FINISHED SIZES

Hat: 3–9 mos (12–18 mos)

Mitts: 3–9 mos (12–18 mos)

FINISHED MEASUREMENTS

Hat: 16½ (18½)" (42 [47]cm) circumference

Mitts: 5½ (7)" (14 [18]cm) circumference

YARN

2 skeins Dale of Norway Baby Ull (100% superwash wool, 50 g, 192 yds [175m])
   color #6714 Aqua (MC)

1 skein Dale of Norway Baby Ull
   color #0010 White (CC)

NEEDLES

16" (41cm) size US 2 (2.75mm) circular needle

1 set of 5 size US 2 (2.75mm) double-pointed needles

GAUGE

32 sts x 44 rows = 4" (10cm) in St st

TECHNIQUES
K2TOG (KNIT 2 TOGETHER):
Dec 1 st by knitting 2 sts tog.

Hat

With MC and size US 2 (2.75mm) circular needle, CO 132 (148) sts. Join for working in the rnd, taking care not to twist sts, and pm at beg of rnd.

Work in k1, p1 rib for 1" (3cm).

Work in St st for 5 (6)" (13 [15]cm), or until piece measures 6 (7)" (15 [18]cm) from cast-on edge.

Divide sts on 2 DPNs—66 (74) sts per needle.

Graft sts from the 2 needles tog using Kitchener st.

✿ NOTE ✿
To graft with Kitchener st, line up both sets of live sts on 2 separate needles with the tips facing the same direction. Thread a yarn needle onto the tail of the back piece. Begin by performing the foll steps once: Bring the needle through the first st on the needle closest to you as if to purl, leaving the st on the needle. Then insert the needle through the first st on the back needle as if to knit, leaving the st on the needle. Now you are ready to graft. * Bring the needle through the first st on the front needle as if to knit, slipping the st off the needle. Bring the needle through the next st on the front needle as if to purl, leaving the st on the needle. Then bring the needle through the first st on the back needle as if to purl, sliding the st off the needle. Bring the needle through the next st on the back needle as if to knit, leaving the st on the needle. Rep from * until all sts are grafted tog. Approx every 2" (5cm), tighten up the sts, starting at the beg of the join. Slip the tip of the yarn needle under each leg of each Kitchener st and pull up gently until the tension is correct. Rep across the entire row of grafted sts. It may help you to say to yourself, "Knit, purl – purl, knit" as you go.

Mitts (make 2)

With MC and size US 2 (2.75mm) DPNs, CO 44 (54) sts. Divide onto 3 DPNs. Join for working in the rnd, pm at beg of rnd.

Work in k1, p1 rib for 1½" (4cm), inc 1 st on last rnd for LARGER SIZE ONLY—44 (55) sts.

Work even in St st for 3 (4)" (8 [10]cm).

DEC FOR TOP OF MITT

RND 1: * K9, k2tog; rep from * to end of rnd—40 (50) sts.

RND 2 AND ALL EVEN-NUMBERED RNDS: Knit.

RND 3: * K8, k2tog; rep from * to end of rnd—36 (45) sts.

RND 5: * K7, k2tog; rep from * to end of rnd—32 (40) sts.

RND 7: * K6, k2tog; rep from * to end of rnd—28 (35) sts.

RND 9: * K5, k2tog; rep from * to end of rnd—24 (30) sts.

RND 11: * K4, k2tog; rep from * to end of rnd—20 (25) sts.

RND 13: * K3, k2tog; rep from * to end of rnd—16 (20) sts.

RND 15: * K2, k2tog; rep from * to end of rnd—12 (15) sts.

RND 17: * K1, k2tog; rep from * to end of rnd—8 (10) sts.

Break yarn, leaving a tail. Thread the yarn tail onto a yarn needle. Draw through rem sts and pull up tight.

FINISHING
Weave in all ends.

With CC and 2 size US 2 (2.75mm) DPNs, cast on 3 sts. Knit 1 row. Slide sts to opposite end of needle. * Pulling yarn across back, knit 1 row. Slide sts to opposite end of needle. Rep from *, creating I-cord. Work 30 (32)" 76 (81)cm of I-cord, or length necessary to fit through wee one's jacket sleeves. Break yarn, pull tight through all sts.

Stitch ends of I-cord to each mitt.

Kangaroo Vest

You've waited too long—the baby shower is this weekend. What will you do? Make this wee vest knit with 100 percent baby alpaca yarn featuring a kangaroo on the move. This is a simple project that will work up quickly, even on US 5 needles. Work the back first, and then look forward to working the kangaroo graphic on the front. Finish off the neck and armholes and you're through!

SIZES
12 mos (18 mos)

FINISHED MEASUREMENTS
Finished chest size: 21 (23)" (53 [58]cm)

Finished length: 11 (12)" (28 [30]cm)

YARN
2 skeins The Fibre Company Savannah DK
(merino/cotton/linen/soya fiber blend, 50 g, 160 yds [146m])
    color Granite (MC)

1 skein The Fibre Company Savannah DK
    color Persimmon (CC)

NEEDLES AND NOTIONS
size US 4 (3.5mm) straight or circular needles

size US 4 (3.5mm) double-pointed needles

size US 5 (3.75mm) straight or circular needles

yarn needle

stitch marker

GAUGE
25 sts x 38 rows = 4" (10cm) in St st with larger needles

ANOTHER GIFT IDEA
Don't forget you can always "transplant" a graphic from one pattern to another. Work the kangaroo into another baby basic, such as a blanket or sweater, or even add it to an adult accessory, such as a hat.

TECHNIQUES
SSK (SLIP, SLIP, KNIT): Dec 1 st by slipping 2 sts knitwise one at a time from the left needle to the right needle. Insert the tip of the left needle into the front of both sts and knit the 2 sts tog.

K2TOG (KNIT 2 TOGETHER): Dec 1 st by knitting 2 sts tog.

Vest

BACK

With MC and size US 4 (3.5mm) needles, CO 67 (73) sts.

ROW 1: * K1, p1; rep from * to last st, k1.

Cont in k1, p1 rib for 5 more rows.

Switch to size US 5 (3.75mm) needles. Work even in St st until piece measures 6 (6½)" 15 (17)cm from cast-on edge, ending with a WS row.

BEGIN ARMHOLE SHAPING

ROWS 1–2: BO 4 sts at beg of next 2 rows—59 (65) sts.

ROW 3 (DEC ROW): K2, SSK, knit to last 4 sts, k2tog, k2—57 (63) sts.

ROW 4: Purl.

ROWS 5–8: Rep Rows 3–4 twice more—53 (59) sts.

ROW 9: Rep Row 3—51 (57) sts.

ROWS 10–12: Work even in St st.

ROW 13: Rep Row 3—49 (55) sts.

ROWS 14–18: Work even in St st.

ROW 19: Rep Row 3—47 (53) sts.

Cont in St st until piece measures 10 (11)" 25 (28)cm from cast-on edge, ending with a WS row.

BEGIN NECK SHAPING
K13 (14), BO 21 (25), k13 (14).

LEFT SHOULDER

ROW 1 (WS): Purl to end of shoulder—13 (14) sts.

ROW 2: BO 3 sts at neck edge, knit to end—10 (11) sts.

ROW 3: Purl to end.

ROW 4: BO 2 sts, knit to end—8 (9) sts.

ROW 5: Purl to end.

ROW 6: K1, SSK, knit to end—7 (8) sts.

ROW 7: Purl to end.

BO rem 7 (8) sts.

RIGHT SHOULDER

Reattach yarn to neck edge of right shoulder.

ROW 1 (WS): Purl to end of shoulder—13 (14) sts.

ROW 2 (RS): Knit to end.

ROW 3: BO 3 sts at neck edge, purl to end—10 (11) sts.

ROW 4: Knit to end.

ROW 5: BO 2, purl to end—8 (9) sts.

ROW 6: Knit to last 3 sts, k2tog, k1—7 (8) sts.

ROW 7: Purl to end.

BO rem 7 (8) sts.

KANGAROO VEST
TO FIT SIZES
12 MOS (18 MOS)

FRONT

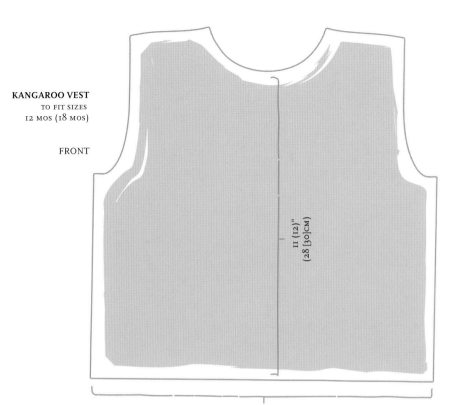

11 (12)" (28 [30]CM)

10½ (11½)" (27 [29]CM)

BACK

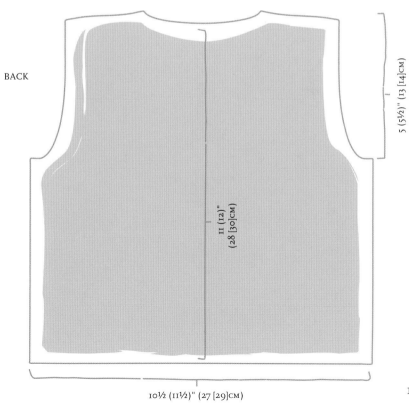

11 (12)" (28 [30]CM)

5 (5½)" (13 [14]CM)

10½ (11½)" (27 [29]CM)

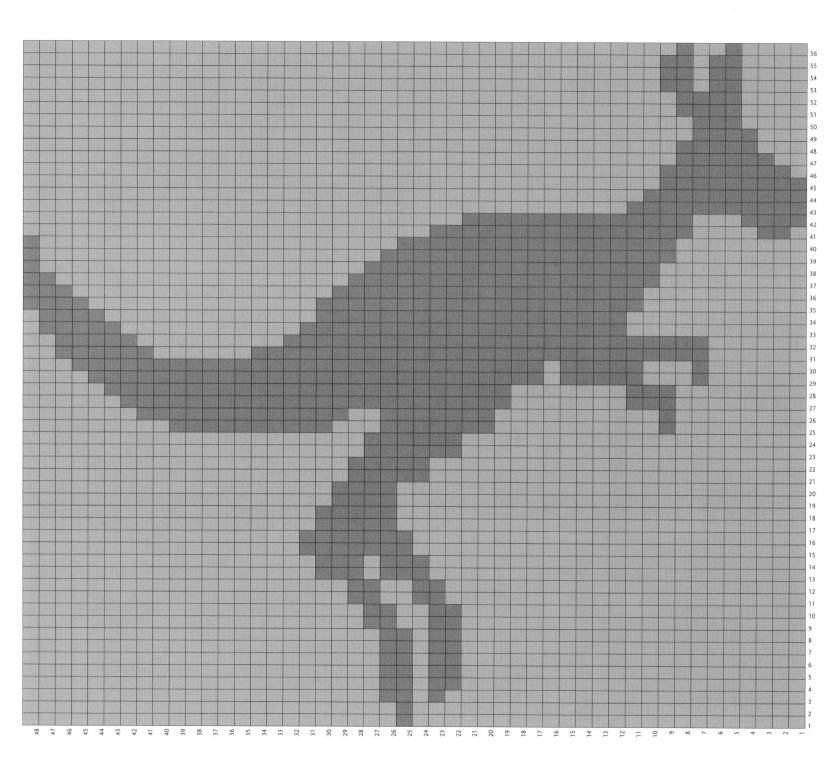

FRONT

Work as for back until piece measures 1¼ (1¾)" (3 [4]cm) from cast-on edge, ending with a WS row.

BEGIN KANGAROO CHART

NOTE

The kangaroo is knitted using the intarsia method and CC yarn. To prevent holes in the work, always twist the 2 yarns at color changes by picking up the new color from under the old and working across to the next color change. Follow chart by knitting RS rows from right to left and WS rows from left to right.

NEXT ROW (RS): With MC, k10 (13) sts, work across 48 sts of chart foll Row 1 from right to left, joining CC where needed, and second ball of MC where needed; end row k9 (12).

Work all 56 rows of chart, keeping it centered on garment as est, and AT THE SAME TIME working armhole shaping as for back until front measures 6 (6½)" (15 [17]cm) from beg.

After armhole shaping is completed, work even in St st until front measures 8½ (9½)" (22 [24]cm) from cast-on edge, ending with a WS row.

BEGIN NECK SHAPING

K18 (19), BO center 11 (15), k18 (19).

LEFT SHOULDER

ROW 1: Purl to neck edge—18 (19) sts.

ROW 2: BO 3, knit to end—15 (16) sts.

ROW 3: Purl to neck edge.

ROW 4: BO 2, knit to end—13 (14) sts.

ROW 5: Purl to neck edge.

ROW 6: K1, SSK, knit to end—12 (13) sts.

ROWS 7–18: Rep this dec EOR 4 times more, then on the foll 4th row 1 time—7 (8) sts.

ROWS 19–21: Work 3 rows even in St st.

BO rem 7 (8) sts.

RIGHT SHOULDER

Reattach yarn at neck edge of right shoulder.

ROW 1: Purl to end—18 (19) sts.

ROW 2: Knit to end.

ROW 3: BO 3 sts, purl to end—15 (16) sts.

ROW 4: Knit to end.

ROW 5: BO 2 sts, purl to end—13 (14) sts.

ROW 6: Knit to last 3 sts, k2tog, k1—12 (13) sts.

ROWS 7–18: Rep this dec EOR 4 times more, then on the foll 4th row 1 time—7 (8) sts.

ROWS 19–21: Work 3 rows even in St st.

BO rem 7 (8) sts.

FINISHING

JOIN FRONT AND BACK

Join shoulder and side seams with mattress st. See the Glossary, page 141, for instructions on working in mattress st.

NECK AND ARMHOLE BANDS

With MC, pick up and knit an even number of sts around neck and armhole openings using size US 2 (2.75mm) DPNs. Mark beg of rnd and join for working in the rnd. Work in k1, p1 rib for 5 rnds. BO loosely in patt.

Weave in all ends. Block.

Heart-Patch Pants

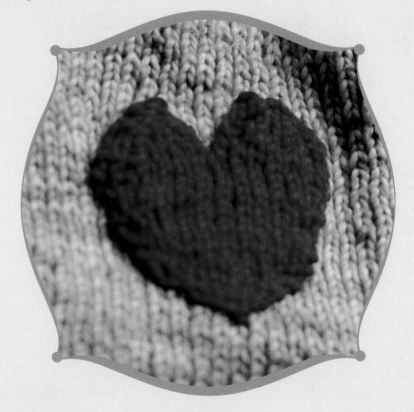

DEPENDING ON THE COLORS AND MOTIFS YOU CHOOSE FOR THESE WEE PANTS, THEY CAN BE PERFECTLY GIRLIE OR ALL BOY. Made with 100 percent cotton and decorated with adorable patches on the knees, these comfy pants are equally great for playtime and dress up. Each leg is knit separately and then joined together to work the waist. The pants are finished off with casing for elastic. The heart patches are created separately then stitched in place.

SIZES
3–6 mos (6–12 mos)

FINISHED MEASUREMENTS
Widest at hip: 22 (24)" (56 [61]cm)

Total length: 13 (15)" (33 [38]cm)

Inside leg: 7 (8)" (18 [20]cm)

Waist to crotch: 6 (7)" (15 [18]cm)

YARN
2 skeins Manos Cotton Stria (Peruvian kettle-dyed cotton, 50 g, 116 yds [106m])
  color #213 pistachio (MC)

1 skein Manos Cotton Stria
  color #217 red (CC)

NEEDLES AND NOTIONS
16" (41cm) size US 6 (4.0mm) circular needle

yarn needle

stitch markers

½" (1cm) wide elastic

GAUGE
18 sts x 28 rows = 4" (10cm) in St st

TECHNIQUES

M1R (MAKE 1 RIGHT): Insert the left needle from back to front into the horizontal strand between the last st worked and the next st on the left needle. Knit this strand through the front loop to twist the st, creating a right-leaning inc.

M1L (MAKE 1 LEFT): Insert the left needle from front to back into the horizontal strand between the last st worked and the first st on the left needle. Knit this strand through the back loop to twist the st, creating a left-leaning inc.

SSK (SLIP, SLIP, KNIT): Dec 1 st by slipping 2 sts knitwise one at a time from the left needle to the right needle. Insert the tip of the left needle into the front of both sts and knit the 2 sts tog.

K2TOG (KNIT 2 TOGETHER): Dec 1 st by knitting 2 sts tog.

P2TOG (PURL 2 TOGETHER): Dec 1 st by purling 2 sts tog.

Pants

LEGS (MAKE 2)
With size US 6 (4.0mm) needles and MC, CO 50 (54) sts.

BEGIN SEED STITCH CUFFS

ROW 1 (RS): * K1, p1; rep to end of row.

ROW 2 (WS): * P1, k1; rep to end of row.

Cont in seed st as est for a total of 10 rows.

Change to St st and work even until leg measures 7 (8)" (18 [20]cm) from cast-on edge. Place sts on a holder.

WAIST
Place sts from both legs on a size US 6 (4.0mm) circular needle to start working in the rnd.

Join yarn at center back, pm to mark beg of rnd. Knit across 25 (27) sts of left leg, pm marking left side, k50 (54) sts, pm to mark right side, knit to end of rnd (center back)—100 (108) sts.

Work in St st for 10 rnds.

DEC RND: Knit to 3 sts before left-side marker, k2tog, k1, sm, k1, SSK, knit to 3 sts before right-side marker, k2tog, k1, sm, k1, SSK, knit to end of rnd—96 (104) sts.

Cont in St st, rep this dec rnd every 7th (8th) rnd 3 times more—84 (92) sts after last dec rnd.

Work even until pants measure 6 (7)" (15 [18]cm) from joining at crotch.

TURNING RIDGE: Purl.

Work in St st for 7 rnds.

BO loosely.

Turn facing in along turning ridge. Stitch into place, leaving a 2" (5cm) opening.

FINISHING
Cut appropriate length of ½" (1cm) wide elastic, allowing extra for seaming. Pin a safety pin to one end of elastic, feed through 2" (5cm) opening of waist casing. Join ends of elastic. Stitch opening closed with yarn needle and yarn.

Weave in all ends.

HEART PATCHES (MAKE 2)

With CC, CO 2 sts.

ROW 1: Purl.

ROW 2 (RS): K1, M1R, M1L, k1—4 sts.

ROW 3: Purl.

ROW 4: K1, M1R, k2, M1L, k1—6 sts.

ROW 5: Purl.

ROW 6: K1, M1R, k4, M1L, k1—8 sts.

ROW 7: Purl.

ROW 8: K1, M1R, k6, M1L, k1—10 sts.

ROWS 9–11: Work even in St st.

ROW 12: K1, M1R, k8, M1L, k1—12 sts.

ROWS 13–15: Work even in St st.

ROW 16: K1, M1R, k10, M1L, k1—14 sts.

ROWS 17–19: Work even in St st.

ROW 20: (Begin knitting top right heart only) K1, SSK, k4, turn—6 sts.

ROW 21: Purl to end.

ROW 22: K1, SSK, k2tog, k1—4 sts.

ROW 23: Purl to end.

ROW 24: SSK, k2tog—2 sts.

ROW 25: P2tog—1 st.

Break yarn, pull tight through rem st.

Reattach yarn to rem 7 sts to knit left top of heart.

ROW 1 (RS): Knit to last 3 sts, k2tog, k1—6 sts.

ROW 2: Purl to end.

ROW 3: K1, SSK, k2tog, k1—4 sts.

ROW 4: Purl to end.

ROW 5: SSK, k2tog—2 sts.

ROW 6: P2tog—1 st.

Break yarn, leaving a long tail for sewing. Pull tight through rem st.

With CC threaded on yarn needle, attach patches to knees. Weave in all ends.

QUICK FIX

Are you thinking to yourself, "Ha! Pants? That sure seems like an awful lot of work"? Why not dress up a pair of store-bought pants by attaching the heart patches and adding an I-cord belt?

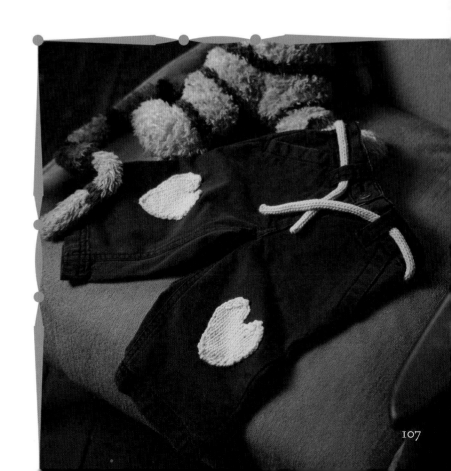

Ducky Cardigan

Two birds adorn the pockets of this cardigan for your dearest wee one. Featuring The Fibre Company's Babe, an alpaca-and-wool blend yarn, it is a squeezably soft garment. Tiny pearl buttons provide closure. Try this perfect shade of blue, suitable for either a girl or a boy.

SIZES
6 mos (12 mos, 18 mos)

FINISHED MEASUREMENTS
Chest circumference: 20½ (21¼, 22)" (52 [54, 56]cm)

Finished length: 11½ (12, 12¼)" (29 [30, 31]cm)

YARN
4 skeins The Fibre Company Babe (alpaca/merino blend, 50 g, 100 yds [91m])
    color #06 Blue Babe (MC)

1 skein The Fibre Company Babe
    color #01 Cream on the Top (CC)

NEEDLES AND NOTIONS
size US 6 (4.0mm) straight or circular needles

size US 7 (4.5mm) straight or circular needles

yarn needle

(6) or (7) buttons, ½" (1cm) in diameter

sewing thread

embroidery thread in orange and black

GAUGE
20 sts x 28 rows = 4" (10cm) in St st with larger needle

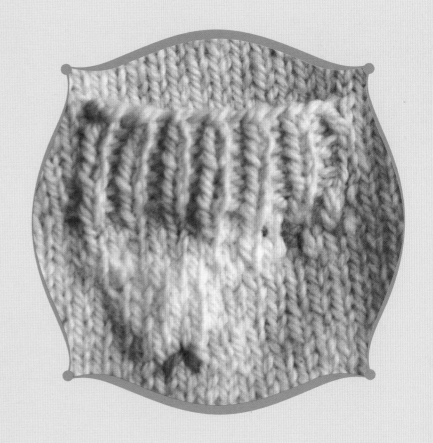

TECHNIQUES

SSK (SLIP, SLIP, KNIT): Dec 1 st by slipping 2 sts knitwise one at a time from the left needle to the right needle. Insert the tip of the left needle into the front of both sts and knit the 2 sts tog.

K2TOG (KNIT 2 TOGETHER): Dec 1 st by knitting 2 sts tog.

P2TOG (PURL 2 TOGETHER): Dec 1 st by purling 2 sts tog.

M1 (MAKE 1): Inc 1 st by picking up, from front to back, the bar between the next st and the st just knit and placing it on the left needle. Knit into the back of the picked-up st.

Cardigan

BACK

With size US 6 (4.0mm) needles and MC, CO 53 (55, 57) sts.

ROW 1: * K1, p1; rep from * to last st, k1.

Cont in k1, p1 ribbing for 1" (3cm), ending with a WS row.

Switch to size US 7 (4.5mm) needles. Work in St st until piece measures 6¾ (7, 7¼)" (17 [18, 18]cm) from beg, ending with a WS row.

BEGIN ARMHOLE SHAPING

BO 2 sts at beg of next 4 rows—45 (47, 49) sts.

NEXT ROW (DEC ROW): K2, SSK, knit to last 4 sts, k2tog, k2—43 (45, 47) sts.

Rep this dec row on the foll 4th row once—41 (43, 45) sts.

Work even in St st until piece measures 10½ (11, 11¼)" (27 [28, 29]cm) from beg, ending with a WS row.

BEGIN NECK SHAPING

PREP ROW: K15 (15, 16); k11 (13, 13) center sts, then place on a holder for back neck; k15 (15, 16).

Work both shoulders at the same time as foll:

ROW 1 (WS): L shoulder: Purl to held sts; R shoulder: Attach another ball of yarn to neck edge of R shoulder. BO 3 (3, 4) sts, purl to end—12 sts (all sizes).

ROW 2 (RS): R shoulder: Knit across; L shoulder: BO 3 (3, 4) sts, knit to end—12 sts.

ROW 3: L shoulder: Purl across; R shoulder: BO 2 (2, 2) sts, purl to end—10 sts.

ROW 4: R shoulder: Knit to last 3 sts, k2tog, k1—9 sts; L shoulder: BO 2 (2, 2) sts, SSK, knit to end—9 sts.

ROW 5: L shoulder: Purl across; R shoulder: Purl across.

ROW 6: R shoulder: BO 3 (3, 3) sts, knit to last 3 sts, k2tog, k1—5 sts; L shoulder: K1, SSK, knit to end—8 sts.

ROW 7: L shoulder: BO 3 (3, 3) sts, purl to end—5 sts; R shoulder: BO rem 5 sts.

ROW 8: L shoulder: BO rem 5 sts.

LEFT FRONT

With size US 6 (4.0mm) needles and MC, CO 24 (25, 26) sts.

Work in k1, p1 ribbing for 1" (3cm), ending with a WS row.

Switch to size US 7 (4.5mm) needles.

Work even in St st for 2" (5cm), ending with a WS row.

Work left front duck chart over next 10 rows with CC yarn, ending with a WS row. Center chart horizontally on rows.

❧ NOTE ❧

Duck chart may be worked using intarsia technique to knit-in duck, or duck may be embroidered in duplicate st after fronts are completed, but before pocket lining is made and sewn down. See the Glossary, page 139, for instructions on working in intarsia.

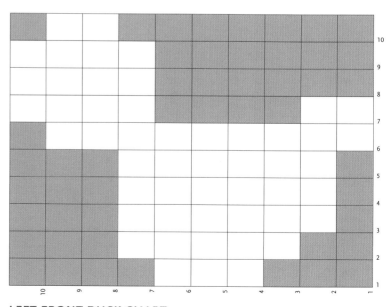

LEFT FRONT DUCK CHART

Work even in St st for 2 rows.

POCKET

K4 (5, 6), place next 14 sts on a holder, CO 14 sts over held sts, k6.

Purl across all sts. Cont in St st until piece measures 6¾ (7, 7¼)" (17 [18, 18]cm), ending with a WS row.

BEGIN ARMHOLE SHAPING

(RS) BO 2 sts at armhole edge on foll 2 RS rows—20 (21, 22) sts.

Purl 1 row even.

NEXT ROW (DEC ROW): K2, SSK, knit to end—19 (20, 21) sts.

Rep this dec row on the foll 4th row once—18 (19, 20) sts.

Work even in St st until piece measures 9 (9¼, 9½)" (23 [23, 24]cm), ending with a RS row.

BEGIN NECK SHAPING

BO 3 sts at neck edge on foll 2 WS rows—12 (13, 14) sts.

NEXT ROW (RS): Knit to last 3 sts, k2tog, k1.

Rep EOR 3 (4, 5) more times—8 sts.

Work even in St st, if necessary, until 2 rows short of total length of back to shoulder. End with a WS row.

NEXT ROW (RS): BO 3, knit to last 3 sts, k2tog, k1—4 sts.

BO rem 4 sts.

RIGHT FRONT

Work as for left front to armhole shaping, working right front duck chart, and ending with a RS row.

BEGIN ARMHOLE SHAPING

(WS) BO 2 sts at armhole edge on foll 2 WS rows—20 (21, 22) sts.

NEXT ROW (DEC ROW, RS): Knit to last 4 sts, k2tog, k2—19 (20, 21) sts.

Rep this dec row on foll 4th row once—18 (19, 20) sts.

Work even in St st until piece measures 9 (9¼, 9½)" (23 [23, 24]cm) from beg, ending with a WS row.

BEGIN NECK SHAPING

BO 3 sts at neck edge on foll 2 RS rows—12 (13, 14) sts.

NEXT ROW: Purl 1 row even.

NEXT ROW (DEC ROW, RS): K1, SSK, knit to end—11 (12, 13) sts.

Rep dec row EOR 3 (4, 5) more times—8 sts.

Work even in St st, if necessary, until 2 rows short of total length of back to shoulder. End with a RS row.

NEXT ROW (WS): BO 3 sts, purl to last 3 sts, p2tog, p1—4 sts.

BO rem 4 sts.

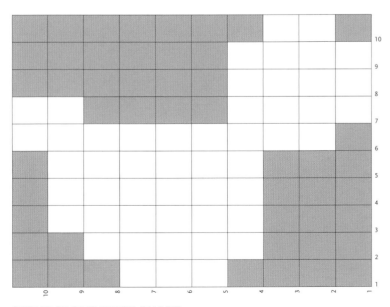

RIGHT FRONT DUCK CHART

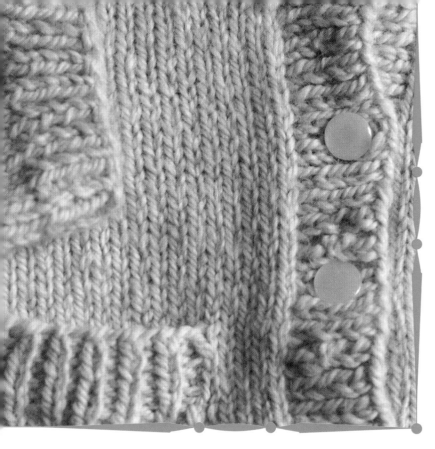

BEGIN CAP SHAPING

BO 2 sts at beg of next 4 rows—34 (34, 36) sts.

NEXT ROW (DEC ROW, RS): K1, SSK, knit to last 3 sts, k2tog, k1—32 (32, 34) sts.

Rep this dec row EOR 9 (9, 10) times more—14 sts.

NEXT ROW: Purl.

BO 2 sts at beg of next 2 rows—10 sts.

BO rem 10 sts.

FINISHING

Sew fronts to back at side seams using mattress st. See the Glossary, page 141, for instructions on working in mattress st.

Sew underarm seams of sleeves. Set in sleeves.

BUTTON BAND

Beg at left front with RS facing and US size 6 (4.0mm) needles, pick up and knit an even number of sts along side of neck rib sts, and down edge of sweater front to bottom of ribbing.

Work in k1, p1 ribbing for 5 rows.

(RS) BO loosely in patt.

Place 6 or 7 markers on button band where you would like to sew buttons.

BUTTONHOLE BAND

Beg at right front with RS facing and size US 6 (4.0mm) needles, pick up and knit same number of sts to match number picked up for left front button band. Pick up sts from bottom edge of sweater ribbing to top front and along side of neck rib sts.

ROW 1 (WS): Work in k1, p1 ribbing.

ROW 2: Cont in k1, p1 rib 1 more row.

ROW 3 (WS): Working in k1, p1 ribbing as est, work 6 or 7 buttonholes spaced to match markers on button band, allowing 3–4 sts above top buttonhole and below bottom buttonhole. Bind off 1 st to match up with indicated spot on button band to create buttonholes.

ROW 4 (RS): Working in ribbing, CO 1 st over each bound-off st, creating buttonholes.

ROW 5: Work 1 more row in ribbing.

BO loosely in patt.

JOIN SHOULDERS

Sew shoulder seams tog.

NECK

With size US 6 (4.0mm) needles and MC, pick up an odd number of sts around neck evenly distributed, including sts from holder.

Work in k1, p1 ribbing for 1" (3cm). BO loosely in rib.

SLEEVES (MAKE 2)

With size US 6 (4.0mm) needles and MC, CO 32 (32, 34) sts.

Work in k1, p1 ribbing for 1" (3cm). Switch to size US 7 (4.5 mm) needles.

INC ROW: K2, m1, knit to last 2 sts, m1, k2—34 (34, 36) sts.

Rep this inc row every 8th row 4 times more—42 (42, 44) sts.

Work even in St st until sleeve measures 6 (6½, 7)" 15 (17, 18)cm, ending with a WS row.

SEW ON BUTTONS AND ADD EMBROIDERED DETAIL

Sew buttons to left button band to correspond with buttonholes on right buttonhole band.

With orange embroidery floss and sewing needle, stitch legs and beak on birds. With black floss, make a French knot for the eye.

FINISH POCKET

Place 14 pocket sts from holder onto size US 6 (4.0mm) needles. Work in k1, p1 ribbing for 1" (3cm). BO loosely. Stitch sides of rib to sweater.

Pick up 14 sts along cast-on edge for pocket lining. Work in St st for 2" (5cm), maintaining same RS rows as sweater body. BO all sts. Stitch lining into place. Weave in all ends.

SLEEVE
6 MOS (12 MOS, 18 MOS)

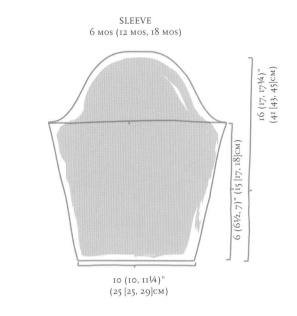

16 (17, 17¾)"
(41 [43, 45]CM)

6 (6½, 7)" (15 [17, 18]CM)

10 (10, 11¼)"
(25 [25, 29]CM)

DUCKY CARDIGAN
TO FIT SIZES 6 MOS (12 MOS, 18 MOS)

FRONT

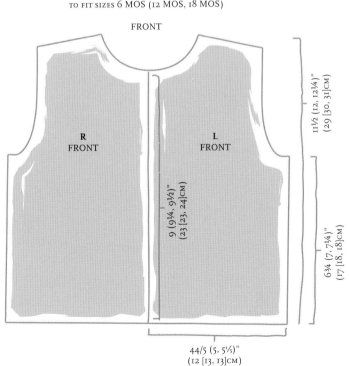

R FRONT

L FRONT

11½ (12, 12¼)"
(29 [30, 31]CM)

9 (9¼, 9½)"
(23 [23, 24]CM)

6¾ (7, 7¼)"
(17 [18, 18]CM)

44/5 (5, 5⅓)"
(12 [13, 13]CM)

BACK

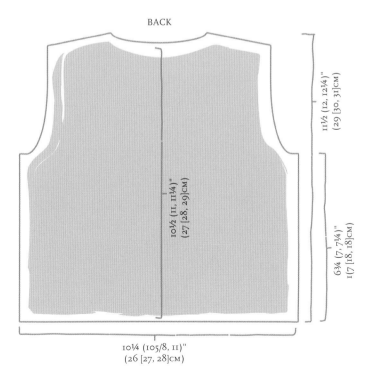

11½ (12, 12¼)"
(29 [30, 31]CM)

10½ (11, 11¼)"
(27 [28, 29]CM)

6¾ (7, 7¼)"
(17 [18, 18]CM)

10¼ (105/8, 11)"
(26 [27, 28]CM)

113

Patchwork Blanket

IF YOU ARE A SMALL-NEEDLE KNITTER, YOU WILL ENJOY MAKING THIS BLANKET. Alternating green and yellow squares are knit in five strips and then sewn together. An apple appliqué is knit separately in three pieces and then sewn to the center square. The blanket is finished with a garter-stitch edge. The featured blanket sports one apple, but you could make as many as you like.

FINISHED MEASUREMENTS
approx 32" x 40" (81cm x 102cm), including border

YARN
4 skeins Dale of Norway Baby Ull (100% superwash wool, 50 g, 192 yds [175m])
> color #2015 Yellow (A)

5 skeins Dale of Norway Baby Ull
> color #8523 Green (B)

1 skein Dale of Norway Baby Ull
> color #4018 Red (C)

1 skein Dale of Norway Baby Ull
> color #3172 Brown (D)

NEEDLES AND NOTIONS
size US 2 (2.75mm) straight or circular needles

1 set of 5 size US 2 (2.75mm) double-pointed needles

yarn needle

GAUGE
28 sts x 40 rows = 4" (10cm) in St st

TECHNIQUES
KFB (KNIT 1 FRONT AND BACK): Inc 1 st by
knitting into the front and back of the next st.

Blanket

STRIPS 1, 3 & 5
With size US 2 (2.75mm) straight or circular needles
and Color A, CO 48 sts.

Work in St st for for 8" (20cm).

SWITCH TO YARN B: Work in St st for 8" (20cm).

SWITCH TO YARN A: Work in St st for 8" (20cm).

SWITCH TO YARN B: Work in St st for 8" (20cm).

SWITCH TO YARN A: Work in St st for 8" (20cm).

BO all sts.

STRIPS 2 & 4
With size US 2 (2.75mm) straight or circular needles
and yarn B, CO 48 sts.

Work in St st for 8" (20cm).

SWITCH TO YARN A: Work in St st for 8" (20cm).

SWITCH TO YARN B: Work in St st for 8" (20cm).

SWITCH TO YARN A: Work in St st for 8" (20cm).

SWITCH TO YARN B: Work in St st for 8" (20cm).

BO all sts.

ASSEMBLE STRIPS
Using mattress st, join the strips in order, from 1–5. See the
Glossary, page 141, for instructions on working in mattress st.

BORDER

SIDE EDGES

ROW 1: With RS facing, using yarn C and size US 2 (2.75mm)
straight or circular needles, pick up and knit evenly along one
side edge of blanket. End off yarn C.

ROWS 2–4: Starting with a WS row and Color B, work in garter
st for 3 rows.

Bind off.

Rep for other side edge.

TOP AND BOTTOM EDGES

ROW 1: With RS facing and using yarn C and size US 2 (2.75mm)
straight or circular needles, pick up and knit evenly across end
of side edge, across top edge and across end of other side edge.
End off yarn C.

ROWS 2–4: Starting with a WS row and yarn B, work in garter
st for 3 rows.

Bind off.

Rep for bottom edge.

Weave in all ends.

Appliqués

APPLE

With yarn C and using size US 2 (2.75mm) straight or circular needles, CO 20 sts.

ROW 1 (RS): Purl.

ROW 2: Kfb in each of first 2 sts, knit to last 2 sts, kfb in each of last 2 sts—24 sts.

ROW 3: Purl.

ROWS 4–7: Rep Rows 2–3 twice more—32 sts.

Work in St st until piece measures 2½" (6cm).

BEG DEC: BO 2 sts at beg of foll 6 rows—20 sts.

BO 20 sts.

LEAF

With yarn B and using size US 2 (2.75mm) needles, CO 8 sts.

ROW 1 (WS): Purl.

ROW 2 (RS): BO 1 st, knit to last st, kfb—8 sts.

ROW 3: Purl.

ROWS 4–9: Rep Rows 2–3 3 times more.

ROW 10: BO 1 st, knit to end—7 sts.

ROW 11: Purl.

ROWS 12–13: Rep Rows 10–11 once more—6 sts.

ROW 14: BO 2 sts, knit to end—4 sts.

ROW 15: Purl.

BO rem sts, leaving a long yarn tail for sewing.

STEM

With 2 size US 2 (2.75mm) DPNs, CO 3 sts. Knit 1 row. Slide sts to opposite end of needle. * Pulling yarn across back, knit 1 row. Slide sts to opposite end of needle. Rep from *, creating I-cord. Make desired length for stem. Break yarn, leaving a long yarn tail for sewing. Pull yarn tail tight through 3 sts to draw up.

FINISHING

Stitch apple into place on center square of blanket. Stitch leaf into place. Stitch stem into place.

Weave in all ends.

QUICK FIX

So maybe knitting a whole blanket on size 3 needles seemed like a good idea when you started it six months ago. But maybe you ran out of time, and maybe the baby is getting close to being a robust one-year-old. Maybe it's time to take the easy way out. Buy a really precious baby blanket, then knit up the apple appliqué with leaf and stem in this pattern and sew it on. Voilá! Your handmade gift is finished in a jiff. Maybe you'll even feel inspired to add multiple appliqués.

Friends

WHEN I THINK ABOUT MY BEST FRIENDS, I REALIZE
HOW I LOVE TO SURROUND MYSELF WITH POSITIVE,
LIVELY PEOPLE. The gifts in this chapter reflect this
uplifting vibe with their bright colors and their fun
function. The sounds of good times and the sense
of joy brought to me by my friends are reflected here
in these five projects.

The *Earflap Hat* (see page 122) is a fast, chunky knit,
and the *Striped Mittens* (see page 126) add playfulness
to even the grayest winter's day. They are both sure to
become popular items among your friends—they will
all want them! The patchwork felted bath mat (see page
134) in vibrant shades of purple is a great addition to your
friend's home. Do you not have much time? The sweet
little *Heart Pin* (see page 120) can be made in under an
hour. Despite its size and speedy make-up, it is a very
meaningful gift. The boutique-style bag (see page 130) is
so fun, and hangs so comfortably over the shoulder, you
won't want to give it away! It can be embellished as much
as you like, so even if you make multiple bags, you can
make each one unique.

Think of the friend, select your project and the
perfect yarn, and go!

Heart Pin

As the inspiration for this gift, I have to give a shout out to Diane of Ferdinand Home Store, here in Portland, Maine. She is always doing something fun with perfectly shaped, perfectly red plastic hearts. I have taken her heart to the knit level with this unique gift that could be created at the very last minute. It can be pinned to a favorite jacket or bag. Recycled plastic provides support to the back, and a cotton ball makes it three-dimensional.

FINISHED MEASUREMENTS
1½" (4cm) tall x 1¼" (3cm) wide

YARN
1 skein Dale of Norway Baby Ull (100% superwash wool, 50 g, 192 yds [175m])
   color #4018 Red

NEEDLES AND NOTIONS
size US 2 (2.75mm) needles

thin plastic, as from produce container

cotton ball

yarn needle

safety pin

TECHNIQUES
KFB (KNIT 1 FRONT AND BACK): Inc 1 st by knitting into the front and back of the next st.

SSK (SLIP, SLIP, KNIT): Dec 1 st by slipping 2 sts knitwise one at a time from the left needle to the right needle. Insert the tip of the left needle into the front of both sts and knit the 2 sts tog.

K2TOG (KNIT 2 TOGETHER): Dec 1 st by knitting 2 sts tog.

P2TOG (PURL 2 TOGETHER): Dec 1 st by purling 2 sts tog.

Heart (make 2)

With size US 2 (2.75mm) needles, CO 4 sts.

Knit 1 row, purl 1 row.

ROW 3: K1, kfb, kfb, k1—6 sts.

ROWS 4 AND 6: Purl.

ROW 5: K1, kfb, knit to last 2 sts, kfb, k1—8 sts.

ROWS 7–12: Rep Rows 5–6—14 sts after Row 12.

Knit 1 row, purl 1 row.

SHAPE RIGHT SIDE OF TOP OF HEART

ROW 1: K1, SSK, k4, turn—6 sts.

ROWS 2–4: Work even in St st.

ROW 5: K1, SSK, k2tog, k1—4 sts.

ROW 6: Purl.

ROW 7: SSK, k2tog—2 sts.

ROW 8: P2tog—1 st.

Break yarn, pull tight through rem st.

SHAPE LEFT SIDE OF TOP OF HEART
Reattach yarn with RS facing.

ROW 1: K4, k2tog, k1—6 sts.

ROWS 2–4: Work even in St st.

ROW 5: K1, SSK, k2tog, k1—4 sts.

ROW 6: Purl.

ROW 7: SSK, k2tog—2 sts.

ROW 8: P2tog—1 st.

Break yarn, pull tight through rem st.

FINISHING
Trace around 1 knit heart onto thin plastic, such as from a produce container. Cut out the heart.

Join the 2 hearts using mattress st. See Glossary, page 141, for instructions on working mattress st. When partway joined, insert plastic heart shape. Insert cotton ball on one side of plastic to puff out front. Finish joining. Attach safety pin through back.

Earflap Hat

THIS HAT IS MADE OUT OF THE FIBRE COMPANY'S PEMAQUID, A SOFT, WARM YARN WITH A BEAUTIFUL SHINE. An incredibly fast project, the finished hat is so hip that once you give it to one friend, you'll be taking orders from others! As a finishing touch, the hat features fun cable ties.

SIZES
One size fits all.

FINISHED MEASUREMENTS
17" (43cm) around (unstretched) by 7¾" (20cm) tall

Cabled ties are 19" (48cm) long

YARN
2 skeins of The Fibre Company Pemaquid (baby alpaca/merino/soy silk blend, 50 g, 60 yds [55m]) in the foll colors:
  color Cranberry (MC)
  color Granite (CC)

NEEDLES AND NOTIONS
16" (41cm) size US 9 (5.5mm) circular needle

16" (41cm) size US 10 (6.0mm) circular needle

1 set of 5 size US 10 (6.0mm) double-pointed needles

GAUGE
16 sts x 24 rows = 4" (10cm) in St st with larger needle

TECHNIQUES
K2TOG (KNIT 2 TOGETHER): Dec 1 st by knitting 2 sts tog.

P2TOG (PURL 2 TOGETHER): Dec 1 st by purling 2 sts tog.

Hat

With size US 10 (6.0mm) circular needle and MC, CO 70 sts. Join for working in the rnd, taking care not to twist sts.

Work in St st for 3½" (9cm)—70 sts.

DEC RND 1: * K8, k2tog; rep from * to end of rnd—63 sts.
Knit 1 rnd.

DEC RND 2: * K7, k2tog; rep from * to end of rnd—56 sts.
Knit 1 rnd.

DEC RND 3: * K6, k2tog; rep from * to end of rnd—49 sts.
Knit 1 rnd.

DEC RND 4: * K5, k2tog; rep from * to end of rnd—42 sts.
Knit 1 rnd.

๑ NOTE ๑
When necessary, switch to size US 10 (6.0mm) DPNs.

DEC RND 5: * K4, k2tog; rep from * to end of rnd—35 sts.
Knit 1 rnd.

DEC RND 6: * K3, k2tog; rep from * to end of rnd—28 sts.
Knit 1 rnd.

DEC RND 7: * K2, k2tog; rep from * to end of rnd—21 sts.
Knit 1 rnd.

DEC RND 8: * K1, k2tog; rep from * to end of rnd—14 sts.
Knit 1 rnd.

DEC RND 9: * K2tog; rep from * to end of rnd—7 sts.
Break yarn, pull tight through rem sts.

With MC and size US 9 (5.5mm) 16" (41cm) circular needle, with RS facing, pick up and knit 70 sts along bottom edge of hat. Pm to mark beg of rnd. Work in k1, p1 rib for 2" (5cm).

NEXT RND: BO 10 sts, work 15 sts in patt, place these 15 sts on a holder, BO 20 sts, work 15 sts in patt, place these 15 sts on a holder, BO rem 10 sts.

EARFLAPS (MAKE 2)
Place 15 earflap sts on size US 9 (5.5mm) needle. Cont working with MC.

ROW 1 (RS): P1, k1, p1, k9, p1, k1, p1—15 sts.

ROW 2: K1, p1, k1, p9, k1, p1, k1.

BEGIN CABLED TIES (MAKE 2)

ROW 3: P1, k2tog, slide 3 sts onto cn, hold in back, k1, k3 from cn, k1, slide 1 st onto cn, hold in front, k3, k1 from cn, k2tog, p1—13 sts.

ROW 4: K1, p11, k1.

ROW 5: P1, k2tog, k7, k2tog, p1—11 sts.

ROW 6: K1, p9, k1.

ROW 7: P1, slide 3 sts onto cn, hold in back, k1, k3 from cn, k1, slide 1 st onto cn, hold in front, k3, k1 from cn, p1.

ROW 8: K1, p9, k1.

ROW 9: P1, k9, p1.

ROWS 10–11: Rep Rows 6–7.

ROW 12: P2tog, purl to last 2 sts, p2tog—9 sts.

Switch to CC.

Work foll 4 rows of cable pattern 28 times, or until tie is desired length:

ROW 1: K9.

ROW 2: P9.

ROW 3: Slide 3 sts onto cn, hold in back, k1, k3 from cn, k1, slide 1 st onto cn, hold in front, k3, k1 from cn—9 sts.

ROW 4: P9.

BO 9 sts.

FINISHING
Weave in all ends.

Striped Mittens

YOUR FRIEND WILL BE GIVING HIGH FIVES ALL AROUND WEARING THESE MITTENS KNITTED WITH THE FIBRE COMPANY'S ORGANIK YARN. This is a fun, fast project fit for a special friend. Create stripes out of as many colors as you want for a real eye-catcher. This mitten is worked flat and then sewn up the side.

FINISHED MEASUREMENTS
10¾" (27cm) high x 8" (20cm) around palm

YARN
2 skeins The Fibre Company Organik (organic wool/
baby alpaca/silk blend, 50 g, 85 yds [78m])
  color #20 Dark Red (A)

1 skein The Fibre Company Organik
  color #180 Blue Stone (B)

NEEDLES AND NOTIONS
size US 7 (4.5mm) straight or circular needles

size US 9 (5.5mm) straight or circular needles

1 set of 5 size US 9 (5.5mm) double-pointed needles

yarn needle

stitch markers

GAUGE
16 sts x 24 rows = 4" (10cm) in St st on larger needles

TECHNIQUES

M1 (MAKE 1): Inc 1 st by picking up, from front to back, the bar between the next st and the st just knit and placing it on the left needle. Knit into the back of the picked-up st.

K2TOG (KNIT 2 TOGETHER): Dec 1 st by knitting 2 sts tog.

SL ST (SLIP STITCH): Insert the tip of the right needle into the first st on the left needle purlwise and slip the st from the left needle to the right needle without knitting it.

Mittens (make 2)

With yarn A and size US 7 (4.5mm) needles, CO 34 sts. Do not join. Mitten will be worked back and forth in rows.

ROW 1: K1, * k2, p2; rep from * to last st, k1.

Cont to work in k2, p2 rib as est for 4" (10cm).

Switch to US size 9 (5.5mm) needles and yarn B.

ROWS 1–2: Work in St st for 2 rows, beg with a knit (RS) row.

BEGIN THUMB GUSSET

ROW 3: K17, pm, m1, k1, m1, pm, knit to end—36 sts.

ROW 4: Purl. Cut yarn B.

ROW 5: With yarn A, k17, sm, m1, k3, m1, sm, knit to end—38 sts.

Drop yarn A, but do not cut. Carry colors loosely up side whenever possible.

ROW 6: With yarn B, purl to marker, sm, with second ball of yarn A, purl gusset sts, sm, with second ball of yarn B, purl to end. (Work sts in between markers in yarn A, now and throughout patt.) Always twist the 2 colors at gusset color change to prevent holes.

ROWS 7–13: Cont to inc 2 sts in thumb gusset on every RS row, keeping entire thumb in yarn A and striping rest of mitten in stripe patt as est with 4 rows yarn B, 1 row yarn A. After Row 13 there will be 13 gusset sts—46 sts total.

ROW 14 (WS): Purl to marker, sl gusset sts to a holder, CO 1 st over thumb, purl to end—34 sts.

✍ NOTE ✍

Remainder of mitten may be worked back and forth on a circular needle without having to cut yarns at color change in striping sequence, by sliding sts to opposite end of needle when other color is needed.

Cont in St st and stripe sequence until mitten measures approx 6" (15cm) from end of ribbing, ending after 4 rows yarn B.

Switch to yarn A for rest of mitten.

BEGIN TOP DECREASES

ROW 1: K1, * k2, k2tog; rep from * to last st, k1—26 sts.

ROW 2: Purl even.

ROW 3: K1, * k1, k2tog; rep from * to last st, k1—18 sts.

ROW 4: Purl even.

ROW 5: K1, * k2tog; rep from * to last st, k1—10 sts.

ROW 6: Purl even.

ROW 7: K2tog across row—5 sts.

Break yarn, leaving a tail. Pull tight through rem sts.

THUMB

With size US 9 (5.5mm) DPNs and yarn A, knit sts from holder plus pick up and knit 1 st over gap at base of thumb—14 sts.

Knit in the rnd on DPNs until thumb measures 1¾" (4cm), or desired length from pick-up point.

DECREASE FOR TOP OF THUMB

RND 1: * K2, k2tog; rep from *, ending k2—11 sts.

RND 2: Knit.

RND 3: * K1, k2tog; rep from *, ending k2—8 sts.

RND 4: K2tog to end of rnd—4 sts.

Break yarn, leaving a tail. Pull tight through rem sts.

FINISHING

Join side seam. Weave in all ends.

Pocket Tote

If I had to pick a favorite weight yarn, it would probably be DK. However, every once in a while it is so satisfying to work a project up in bulky weight yarn. I especially love working with Blue Sky Alpacas Bulky Hand Dyes. This yarn has a wonderful hand and comes in great colors. This bag is nice and big, but thanks to the big gauge it doesn't take long to make. Featuring a functional pocket, it's a bag to be used daily. You can line it with fabric to give it extra durability.

FINISHED MEASUREMENTS
approx 15" (38cm) high, excluding handles

18" (46cm) wide at top

YARN
6 skeins Blue Sky Alpacas Bulky Hand Dyes (alpaca/wool blend, 100 g, 45 yds [41m])
    color #1011 Teal (MC)

1 skein Blue Sky Alpacas Bulky Hand Dyes
    color #1023 Daffodil (CC1)

2 skeins Blue Sky Alpacas Bulky Hand Dyes
    color #1022 Spearmint (CC2)

NEEDLES AND NOTIONS
size US 15 (10mm) 24" (61cm) circular needle

yarn needle

(1) 1½" to 2" (4cm to 5cm) button

(4) 1" (3cm) buttons (optional)

fabric to line bag (optional)

GAUGE
8 sts x 12 rows = 4" (10cm) in St st

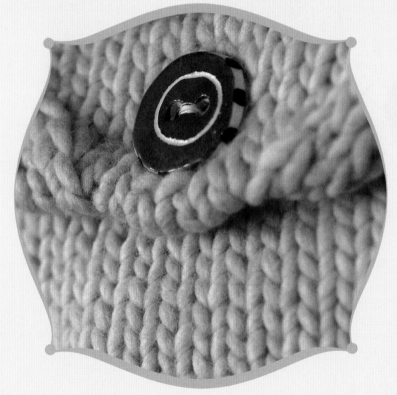

TECHNIQUES

M1 (MAKE 1): Inc 1 st by picking up, from front to back, the bar between the next st and the st just knit and placing it on the left needle. Knit into the back of the picked-up st.

SSK (SLIP, SLIP, KNIT): Dec 1 st by slipping 2 sts knitwise one at a time from the left needle to the right needle. Insert the tip of the left needle into the front of both sts and knit the 2 sts tog.

K2TOG (KNIT 2 TOGETHER): Dec 1 st by knitting 2 sts tog.

P2TOG (PURL 2 TOGETHER): Dec 1 st by purling 2 sts tog.

Bag (make 2 pieces)

With MC and size US 15 (10mm) needles, CO 30 sts.

Work in St st for 4 rows.

INC ROW: K2, m1, knit to last 2 sts, m1, k2—32 sts.

Cont in St st, rep Inc Row on foll 7th row once, then on foll 12th row 3 times—40 sts.

Purl 1 row.

TURNING RIDGE: Purl 1 row on RS.

Place sts on a holder.

Join front and back along bottom edge with mattress st. See the Glossary, page 141, for instructions on working in mattress st.

TOP FACING

Place front and back sts from holders on size US 15 (10mm) circular needle.

Join for working in the rnd. Pm for beg of rnd. With CC1, work in St st for 4 rnds.

BO loosely, leaving a long tail for sewing. Turn facing to inside top of bag and sew in place.

POCKET

With CC1 and size US 15 (10mm) needles, CO 10 sts.

Work 2 rows in St st.

INC ROW: K1, m1, knit to last st, m1, k1—12 sts.

Purl 1 row.

Rep last 2 rows twice more—16 sts.

Cont in St st until pocket measures 5" (13cm), ending with a WS row.

TURNING RIDGE: Purl 1 row across RS.

Work 3 rows in St st.

BO loosely, leaving a long tail for sewing. Fold facing to pocket inside at turning ridge and sew in place.

FLAP

With CC2 and size US 15 (10mm) needle, CO 16 sts.

ROWS 1–4: Work in St st for 4 rows.

CREATE BUTTONHOLE

ROW 5: K7, BO 2, k7.

ROW 6: P7, CO 2, p7.

ROW 7: K2, SSK, knit to last 4 sts, k2tog, k2—14 sts.

ROW 8: P2, p2tog, purl to last 4 sts, p2tbl, p2—12 sts.

ROW 9: K2, SSK, knit to last 4 sts, k2tog, k2—10 sts.

BO loosely.

∾ NOTE ∾

To prevent the pocket flap from curling up, you may want to work a single crochet border around the flap.

STRAPS (MAKE 2)

With MC and size US 15 (10mm) needles, CO 5 sts.

Work even in St st until piece measures 26" (66cm), or desired length, ending with a WS row.

TURNING RIDGE: Purl 1 row on RS.

Switch to CC2. Cont in St st until entire strap measures 52" (132cm), or desired length.

BO. Fold along turning ridge. Join sides of strap using mattress st, forming a tube.

FINISHING

Stitch pocket and pocket flap into place.

Attach button, lining it up with button hole.

Stitch straps securely to bag. Embellish bottom of straps with optional buttons if desired.

Birdie Felted Patchwork Bath Mat

MAKE THIS SWEET BATH MAT FOR SOME TWEET TWEET UNDER YOUR FEET. It makes a great gift for friends. This mat is worked in two strips that are joined together and felted. You may follow the example shown here or add your own personal touches.

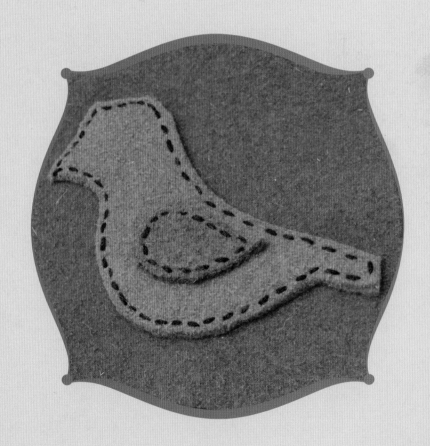

FINISHED MEASUREMENTS
Before felting: 25" x 61" (64cm x 155cm)
After felting: approx 16" x 32" (41cm x 81cm)

YARN
1 skein Cascade 220 (100% Peruvian Highland wool, 100 g, 220 yds [201m]) in each of the foll colors:
  color #8909 (A)
  color #8901 (B)
  color #7803 (C)
  color #9424 (D)
  color #9474 (E)
  color #7822 (F)

NEEDLES AND NOTIONS
size US 9 (5.5mm) straight or circular needles

yarn needle

GAUGE
17 sts x 24 rows = 4" (10cm) in St st (before felting)

Bath Mat

STRIP 1

With size US 9 (5.5mm) needles, CO 53 sts with yarn A.

Work in St st for 92 rows.

SWITCH TO YARN B: Work in St st for 92 rows.

SWITCH TO YARN C: Work in St st for 92 rows.

SWITCH TO YARN D: Work in St st for 92 rows.

Bind off.

STRIP 2

With size US 9 (5.5mm) needles, CO 53 sts with yarn B.

Work in St st for 92 rows.

SWITCH TO YARN C: Work in St st for 92 rows.

SWITCH TO YARN D: Work in St st for 92 rows.

SWITCH TO YARN E: Work in St st for 92 rows.

Bind off.

SQUARE FOR BIRD CUTOUTS

With size US 9 (5.5mm) needles, CO 53 sts with yarn A.

Work in St st for 150 rows.

BO.

SQUARE FOR WING CUTOUTS

With size US 9 (5.5mm) needles, CO 53 sts with yarn E.

Work in St st for 40 rows.

BO.

FINISHING

Join strips 1 and 2 using mattress st. See the Glossary, page 141, for instructions on working in mattress st.

FELTING

Place joined strips and squares for bird and wing cutouts in a top-loading washing machine. Fill machine with hot water and allow to agitate until pieces are well felted. You may need to turn the dial back to agitate through several cycles. Spin dry. Lay flat to dry thoroughly.

Cut out bird and wing appliqué templates on this page. Trace around the templates onto the felted squares you made for the bird and wing. Cut them out. Stitch the bird and wing to the bath mat as shown using yarn F.

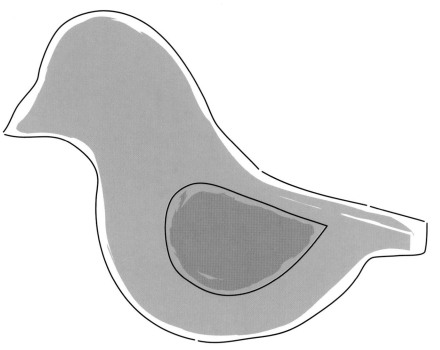

Template for bird and wing appliqué shown at full size.

QUICK FIX

If you're thinking, "Cute, but no way am I going to knit all that just so I can shrink it," there is an easier way. A couple of easier ways, actually. You can make the bath ma by felting old sweaters and cutting them into squares. Join the squares with sewing thread, and you'll be finished in no time. For a special touch, attach appliqués as for the original design. This pattern also works great as a table runner. Reduce it to one strip instead of two joined strips, and make it one square shorter.

Knitting Resources

Knitting Abbreviations

beg	BEGINNING
BO	BIND OFF
C4L	CABLE 4 LEFT
C4R	CABLE 4 RIGHT
CC	CONTRAST COLOR
cn	CABLE NEEDLE
CO	CAST ON
dec	DECREASE
DPN(s)	DOUBLE-POINTED NEEDLE(S)
EOR	END OF ROW/ROUND
foll	FOLLOWING
inc	INCREASE
k	KNIT
kfb	KNIT 1 FRONT AND BACK
k2tog	KNIT 2 TOGETHER
k3tog	KNIT 3 TOGETHER
m1	MAKE ONE
MC	MAIN COLOR
p	PURL
pm	PLACE MARKER
p2tog	PURL 2 TOGETHER
p3tog	PURL 3 TOGETHER
psso	PASS SLIPPED STITCH OVER
rem	REMAINING
RS	RIGHT SIDE
rep	REPEAT
SKP	SLIP, KNIT, PASS
sl	SLIP
sm	SLIP MARKER
SSK	SLIP, SLIP, KNIT
st(s)	STITCH(ES)
work 2 tog	WORK 2 TOGETHER
WS	WRONG SIDE
w&t	WRAP AND TURN
wyib	WITH YARN IN BACK
wyif	WITH YARN IN FRONT
yo	YARN OVER

Yarn Weight Guidelines

Because the names given to different weights of yarn can vary widely depending on the country of origin or the yarn manufacturer's preference, The Craft Yarn Council of America has put together a standard yarn weight system to impose a bit of order on the sometimes unruly yarn labels. Look for a picture of a skein of yarn with a number 1–6 on most kinds of yarn to figure out its "official" weight. Gauge is given over Stockinette stitch. The information in the chart below is taken from www.yarnstandards.com.

	SUPER BULKY (6)	BULKY (5)	MEDIUM (4)	LIGHT (3)	FINE (2)	SUPERFINE (1)	LACE (0)
TYPES OF YARN IN CATEGORY	bulky, roving	chunky, craft, rug	worsted, afghan, aran	dk, light, worsted	sport, baby	sock, fingering, baby	fingering, 10-count crochet thread
STITCHES PER 4" (10CM)	6–11 sts	12–15 sts	16–20 sts	21–24 sts	23–26 sts	27–32 sts	33–40 sts
US NEEDLE SIZE	11 and larger	9 to 11	7 to 9	5 to 7	3 to 5	1 to 3*	000 to 1

* Lace-weight yarns are generally paired with larger needles to create a lacy, openwork pattern. Follow the gauge given in the pattern.

Substituting Yarns

If you substitute yarn, be sure to select a yarn of the same weight as the yarn recommended for the project. Even after checking that the recommended gauge on the yarn you plan to substitute is the same as for the yarn listed in the pattern, make sure to knit a swatch to ensure that the yarn and needles you are using will produce the correct gauge.

Quick Reference

Sometimes you need a little help or inspiration to get you through a tough spot or to get you going. Here are some of the books and Web sites I turn to again and again for patterns, techniques and ideas.

DESIGN HELP...

Vogue Knitting: The Ultimate Knitting Book
by Sixth & Spring Books

Vogue Knitting Stitchionary Volume One, Knit & Purl
by Sixth & Spring Books

Knitting on the Edge
by Nicky Epstein

Sweater Design in Plain English
by Maggie Righetti

INSPIRATION AND GREAT PATTERNS...

Alterknits: Imaginative Projects and Creativity Exercises
by Leigh Radford and John Rizzo

Fitted Knits: 25 Designs for the Fashionable Knitter
by Stefanie Japel

Handknits for Kids: 25 Original Designs for Girls and Boys
by Lucinda Guy and Francois Hall

Knit 2 Together
by Tracey Ullman & Mel Clark

Loop-d-Loop: More than 40 Novel Designs for Knitters
by Teva Durham and Adrian Buckmaster

ONLINE GEMS...

Knit Pro
Take your favorite image and transform it into a knitting graph. Super-easy to use—and free!
www.microrevolt.org/knitPro

Knitty
A source of substance for free knitting patterns.
www.knitty.com

Glossary

CABLES

Cabling is a technique used to cross one group of stitches in front of another. Cables are created by slipping a prescribed number of stitches onto a cable needle and holding the needle to the front or the back of the work, then knitting a certain number of stitches from the left needle. The held stitches are then knitted from the cable needle and the row continues as usual. The number in the abbreviation is the total number of stitches involved in the cable. Divide the number in half to know how many stitches to slip to the cable needle and how many to knit from the left needle. For example, follow instructions to "C4F" (cable four front) by slipping two stitches to a cable needle and holding them in front of the work, then knit two stitches from the left needle. Finish the cable by knitting the two held stitches from the cable needle. This creates a four-stitch cable that crosses to the left.

COLOR WORK

INTARSIA
At each color change, yarns must be wrapped around each other at the back of the work to prevent holes in the fabric. You may work with separate skeins, with yarn wound on bobbins, or with very long strands of yarn. Take time to untangle your strands every few rows. Work charts from right to left beginning with the row numbered "1."

STRIPES
When working stripes that are two to four rows apart, do not break the yarn when switching colors. Instead, carry the unused color up the side of the knitting and wrap the working yarn around it one time loosely at the beginning of the row.

SLIP, SLIP, KNIT (SSK)

To create a left-slanting decrease, slip the first stitch as if to knit, slip the second stitch as if to knit, and then insert the left needle into the front of both stitches and knit them together.

I-CORD

To make I-cord, cast on a small number of stitches, three or four works best, to one DPN. Knit one row. Slide the stitches to the opposite end of the needle. * Pulling the yarn across the back, knit one row. Slide the stitches to the opposite end of the needle. Repeat from *, creating I-cord. When you reach the desired length, break the yarn, pulling it tight through all stitches. Weave the end of the yarn back through the tube. Sew the end of the I-cord to an earflap or mitten cuff to make a handy tie. Or graft the I-cord to knitted fabric with mattress stitch as a decorative element.

INCREASES

KNIT ONE IN FRONT AND BACK (KFB)

An easy way to increase is to knit one in the front and back of a stitch (kfb). To make this type of increase, simply insert your right-hand needle into the next stitch on the left-hand needle and knit the stitch, keeping the stitch on the left-hand needle instead of sliding it off. Then bring your right-hand needle around to the back, knit into the back loop of the same stitch, and slip both stitches off the needle.

MAKE ONE (M1)

Unless otherwise indicated, perform make one (m1) knitwise. Some patterns do call for making one purlwise so the added stitch blends in seamlessly with the rest of the row.

M1 (MAKE 1): Increase one stitch by picking up, from front to back, the bar between the next stitch and the stitch just knit and placing it on the left needle. Knit into the back of the picked-up stitch.

M1 PURLWISE (MAKE 1 PURLWISE): Increase one stitch by picking up, from back to front, the bar between the next stitch and the stitch just knit and placing it on the left needle. Knit into the front of the picked-up stitch.

PICKING UP STITCHES

To pick up a stitch, insert the tip of one needle through the side of a stitch from front to back. Leaving about a 3" to 4" (8cm to 10cm) tail, wrap the yarn around the needle as you would for a regular knit stitch. Bring the yarn through the stitch, creating a

Glossary Continued

DECREASES

KNIT TWO TOGETHER (K2TOG)

Knitting two stitches together as one (k2tog) is a simple way to decrease the number of stitches in a row, creating a right-slanting decrease. Simply slip your right-hand needle through the first two stitches on the left-hand needle from front to back, as for a regular knit stitch. Knit the two stitches as one, creating one less stitch. To knit three together (k3tog), perform the same operation with three stitches instead of two.

PURL TWO TOGETHER (P2TOG)

Slip your right-hand needle through the first two stitches on the left-hand needle from back to front, as for a regular purl stitch. Purl the two stitches as one, creating one less stitch and a right-slanting decrease from the Right Side of the work. To purl three together (p3tog), perform the same operation with three stitches instead of two.

loop on your needle. This loop is the first picked-up stitch. Continue to pick up the number of stitches required, making sure to space them evenly.

PLACING AND SLIPPING A MARKER (PM AND SM)

Sometimes a pattern calls for you to place a marker (pm) and slip a marker (sm). Markers are generally small plastic rings that slide onto a needle and rest between stitches, marking a certain spot. If you don't have markers on hand, cut small pieces of scrap yarn in a contrasting color. Tie the scrap yarn around the needle in the indicated spot in a loose knot. Move the marker from one needle to the other when you come to it. Continue as usual.

SEAMING

Two main methods are used to seam knitted pieces together in this book. Mattress stitch is used to seam pieces with bound-off edges together, or to seam pieces together along their sides. Kitchener stitch is used to graft two rows of live stitches together. Both methods create a seamless join from the right side, and Kitchener stitch is seamless from both the front and back of the work.

Kitchener Stitch (kitchener st)
To graft with Kitchener stitch, line up both sets of live stitches on two separate needles with the tips facing the same direction. Thread a yarn needle onto the tail of the back piece. Begin by performing the following steps once: Bring the needle through the first stitch on the needle closest to you as if to purl, leaving the stitch on the needle. Then insert the needle through the first stitch on the back needle as if to knit, leaving the stitch on the needle. Now you are ready to graft. * Bring the needle through the first stitch on the front needle as if to knit, slipping the stitch off the needle. Bring the needle through the next stitch on the front needle as if to purl, leaving the stitch on the needle. Then bring the needle through the first stitch on the back needle as if to purl, sliding the stitch off the needle. Bring the needle through the next stitch on the back needle as if to knit, leaving the stitch on the needle. Rep from * until all the stitches are grafted together. Approximately every 2" (5cm), tighten up the stitches, starting at the beginning of the join. Slip the tip of the yarn needle under each leg of each Kitchener stitch and pull up gently until the tension is correct. Repeat across the entire row of grafted stitches. It may help you to say to yourself, "Knit, purl – purl, knit" as you go.

Mattress Stitch (mattress st)
You'll work mattress stitch differently depending on whether you are seaming vertically or horizontally. For both vertical-to-vertical and horizontal-to-horizontal seaming, you'll begin the same way. Place the blocked pieces side-by-side with right sides facing. With yarn needle and yarn, insert the needle from back to front through the lowest corner stitch of one piece, then in the lowest corner stitch of the opposite piece, pulling the yarn tight to join the two pieces.

To work vertical-to-vertical mattress stitch, work back and forth as follows: On the first piece, pull the edge stitch away from the second stitch to reveal a horizontal bar. Insert the needle under the bar and pull through. Insert the needle under the parallel bar on the opposite piece and pull through. Continue in this manner, pulling the yarn tight every few rows. Weave the end into the wrong side of the fabric.

To work horizontal-to-horizontal mattress stitch, work back and forth as follows: With bound-off stitches lined up stitch-for-stitch, insert the needle under the first stitch inside the bound-off edge to one side and pull it through, then under the parallel stitch on the other side and pull it through. Continue in this manner, pulling the yarn tight every few rows. Weave the end into the wrong side of the fabric.

SHORT ROWS

When a pattern includes short rows, you will be working partial rows, knitting or purling only a certain number of stitches before wrapping the yarn and turning the work midway through the row. Short rows create unique effects in knitted fabric, including causing the piece to swirl in a circle or to ripple. To work short rows, you'll need to perform the following two operations.

(RS) WRAP AND TURN (W&T): On the Right Side of the work, and with the yarn in front, slip one stitch from the left needle to the right. Move the yarn to the back, slip the stitch back to the left needle, turn work. One stitch has been wrapped.

(WS) WRAP AND TURN (W&T): On the Wrong Side of the work, and with the yarn in back, slip one stitch from the left needle to the right. Move the yarn to the front, slip the stitch back to the left needle, turn work. One stitch has been wrapped.

Whenever you come to a wrap, work the wrap together with the stitch it wraps. To pick up a wrap and its stitch, slide the tip of the right needle into the wrap from the front of the work and place the wrap on the left needle alongside the stitch it wraps. Knit the two loops together as one stitch.

Resources

It's a good time to be a knitter. There are many wonderful yarns available to handknitters today. You probably have a favorite local yarn shop or two, and of course there is always the wide world of the Internet. If you have trouble finding exactly what you want, use the manufacturer information provided here to find local and online vendors.

ALPACA WITH A TWIST
4272 Evans Jacobi Road
Georgetown, IN 47122
866.37TWIST
www.alpacawithatwist.com

BLUE SKY ALPACAS
P.O. Box 88
Cedar, MN 55011
888.460.8862
www.blueskyalpacas.com

BROWN SHEEP COMPANY, INC.
100662 County Road 16
Mitchell, NE 69357
800.826.9136
www.brownsheep.com

CASCADE YARNS
www.cascadeyarns.com

CLASSIC ELITE YARNS
122 Western Avenue
Lowell, MA 01851-1434
978.453.2837
www.classiceliteyarns.com

DALE OF NORWAY
4750 Shelburne Road,
Suite 20
Shelburne, VT 05482
802.383.0132
www.daleofnorway.com

THE FIBRE COMPANY
North Dam Mill
Two Main Street
Biddeford, ME 04005
207.282.0734
www.thefibreco.com

FROG TREE
Frog Tree T&C Imports
P.O. Box 1119
East Dennis, MA 02641
508.385.8862
www.frogtreeyarns.com

KARABELLA YARNS
800.550.0898
www.karabellayarns.com

KNITWIT YARN SHOP
247A Congress Street
Portland, ME 04101
207.774.6444
www.yarnonthebrain.com

LORNA'S LACES
4229 North Honore Street
Chicago, IL 60613
773.935.3803
www.lornaslaces.net

MANOS DEL URUGUAY YARNS
www.manos.com.uy

NORO
www.noroyarns.com

PEACE FLEECE
475 Porterfield Road
Porter, ME 04068
www.peacefleece.com

ROWAN YARNS
Westminster Fibers
4 Townsend West, Unit 8
Nashua, NH 03063
800.445.9276
www.knitrowan.com

Index

Check out these other fabulous knitting and crochet titles from North Light Books.

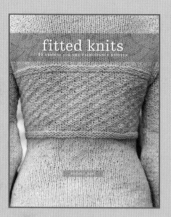

FITTED KNITS
BY STEFANIE JAPEL

Fitted Knits features 25 projects to fit and flatter. You'll learn how to tailor T-shirts, sweaters, cardigans, coats and even a skirt and a dress to fit you perfectly. Take the guesswork out of knitting garments that fit. The book includes a detailed section that shows you how to know when and where increases and decreases should be placed to create the most attractive shaping.

ISBN-13: 978-1-58180-872-8
ISBN-10: 1-58180-872-0
paperback, 144 pages, Z0574

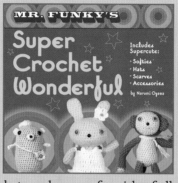

MR. FUNKY'S SUPER CROCHET WONDERFUL
BY NARUMI OGAWA

Mr. Funky's Super Crochet Wonderful is filled with 25 supercute crochet patterns for adorable Japanese-style stuffed animals and accessories. You'll find candy-color elephants, panda bears, kitty cats, hamsters and even a snake, plus fashionable hats and purses for girls of all ages. Each pattern features written instructions as well as traditional Japanese crochet diagrams.

ISBN-13: 978-1-58180-966-4
ISBN-10: 1-58180-966-2
paperback, 112 pages, Z0697

SOFT + SIMPLE KNITS FOR LITTLE ONES
BY HEIDI BOYD

Learn to knit simple, adorable projects for the little ones in your life using the basic techniques taught in this book. *Soft + Simple Knits for Little Ones* includes patterns for clothing, accessories and toys that can be knit for last-minute gifts or for nearly instant gratification. Even if you've never picked up a set of knitting needles, author Heidi Boyd will teach you the skills needed to quickly and successfully complete each of the projects in this book without spending too much money or too much time.

ISBN-13: 978-1-58180-965-7
ISBN-10: 1-58180-965-4
paperback, 160 pages, Z0696

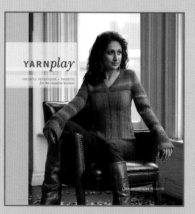

YARNPLAY
BY LISA SHOBHANA MASON

YarnPlay shows you how to fearlessly mix yarns, colors and textures to create bold and graphic handknits. You'll learn how to draw from your yarn stash to create stylish, colorful knits, including sweaters, tanks, hats, scarves, blankets, washcloths and more for women, men and children. Best of all, you'll learn knitting independence—author Lisa Shobhana Mason believes in learning the rules so you can break them. She teaches you how to take a pattern and make it your own.

ISBN-13: 978-1-58180-841-4
ISBN-10: 1-58180-841-0
paperback, 128 pages, Z0010

These books and other fine North Light titles are available at your local craft retailer, bookstore or from online suppliers.